MW00780480

ISBN: 0-9714086-9-6

Published by Tarbutton Press

SAN: 254-4989

http://www.tarbuttonpress.com

Manufactured in the United States of America.

Pawprints Upon My Heart

By
Mary Garwood

DEDICATION

I dedicate Pawprints Upon My Heart to my father,

Fred J. Kullberg,

for when it came to the treatment of animals,

he taught me my heart.

From – **"The One Who Knows"**

Whenever my broken heart sighs,

Four Paws looks upon me with molten eyes.

You see my old friend,

I will know your love until my very end.

-Fredrick Hall Marler

FOREWORD

Dear Reader,

This book is not simply about animal companions. It is really about love, compassion, hope, and faithfulness-- those basic humane virtues and values that let us discover in our many relationships truths about ourselves and others. More importantly, we are able to experience the self-transformation that happens when we meet that "special someone."

"PAWPRINTS UPON MY HEART" relates in many poignant ways how important all our relationships are, both animal and human. It reminds us how often we are touched by those around us. As you read 'PAWPRINTS,' be prepared for your heart to be invigorated by the knowledge that our companion animals, and for that matter all animals, deserve our protection. They are an essential part of our lives-- touching each of us in a very special and unique way.

Humanely yours,

Timothy M. O'Brien

President

American Humane Association

AUTHOR BIOGRAPHY

-by her husband-

A traditional author's biography would begin by recognizing Mary as a middle-aged, suburban housewife who has ultimately and inescapably arrived to the realization that life really does begin after 40. But there's nothing traditional about Mary, so let's tell it like it is...the story of the 'keeper of the zoo.'

I first met Mary while hiring her as a lifeguard when she was but a teenager. Almost immediately I recognized her as not only being an outstanding athlete, but as an up beat, always positive thinking individual of multitudinous interests. That having been said, let's skip into the next time zone.

One day while explaining do, re, mi, fa, so, la, ti, do, to her private music students, another of her pupils tearfully approached her with an injured bird and asked Mary if she would be willing to care for it. In no time at all, the bird had practically become a member of the family, and in less time yet, came another bird and then others. The children of the neighborhood soon knew her, as 'The Bird Lady' and our home had become an aviary filled with bird songs.

At that same time, a Veterinarian friend determined if Mary could work such wonders with birds, what might she have to offer to the many other orphaned and injured wildlife creatures brought to his animal hospital? Soon it was a raccoon here-- a squirrel there-- an opossum! Was it any wonder I became a state licensed animal rehabilitator (with Mary serving in the capacity of head nurse)?

Did this young mother of three have too much time on her hands or what? Wasn't there enough to do in her capacity of mother, housewife, home gardener, plumber, carpenter, painter, and music teacher— not to mention college classes? Apparently not, for she then purchased a Baskin Robbins 31 flavors Ice Cream store. (P.S.) She is now writing an electrifying book on those experiences.

You see, reading, writing animal stories and children's books, became another addition to Mary's pastime experiences, but that special angel of light-- that heavenly sent guardian of animals was still there for those *critters* in need. Today, the 'Edgewood House' is not only a permanent home to two dogs and nine cats, it is a halfway house for any creature great or small-- and none are turned away.

It is therefore no wonder those narratives and anecdotes of her diaries, which chronicled each character having touched her life, became the substance of *"Pawprints Upon (her) Heart,"* experiences-- which have now found a place in the hearts of other animal lovers.

And what about the Mary of today? Well, four grandchildren later, she's that same wonderful person she has always been known to be. She spends much of her *leisurely* time volunteering at Rockford's Arlington Animal Cemetery. It is there, where she designed a 150'x25' 'Rainbow Ridge' hillside garden. This botanical collage from which thousands of brightly colored annuals and perennials now embellishes the burial sights where once living pets who shared life's happiest moments with their people families have been tenderly placed to their eternal rest.

To any reader of "*Pawprints Upon My Heart,*" – to anyone who has ever called an animal, "Friend," they will soon relate to Mary and her genuine animal aficionado and understand why those who know her best refer to her as the one who **talks to animals.**

ACKNOWLEDGEMENTS

"You've got to have a dream, if you don't have a dream, how you gonna have a dream come true?"

Happy Talk from South Pacific

The words from this song kept reminding me that pursuing my goal was the only way a dream was to become an actuality. That dream was to see Pawprints published and in the hands of those who are proud to belong to the brotherhood and sisterhood of devoted animal lovers. This book is my way of documenting the lives of the animals that so deeply touched my heart and to assure a lasting tribute to them as their stories now 'belong to the ages'.

First thanks must go to husband, Ben. His compassion for misfortunate animals is all encompassing and his dedication to helping them is limitless. He watched as individual stories developed into a book and gave advice, guidance, and encouragement. I am extremely grateful for his support and contributions but greatest of all is the fact he understood my need to bring in our eight stray cats. A dog person by nature, he seemed to realize that cats provided the solace that was missing from my soul. The giving of this gift out-shadows every other gesture of kindness bestowed upon me in my life.

After the initial shock that a 'mom' was actually capable of doing more than cooking, laundry, cleaning and taking care of others—my children Ginger, Gigi, and Clint became my great cheerleaders. They offered personal insights, remembered long forgotten facts and

9

recalled memories that helped embellish the stories. Clint was invaluable with editing, marketing and PR.

Jeanne Marler, long-time friend and confidant was the person who truly understood what writing this journal has meant to me. She is my mentor, cat-lover comrade and believer in all things possible.

A gracious thank-you to my personal reading club who followed the growth of Pawprints chapter by chapter. They are Fred and Jeanne Marler, Jun Zhou, Carol Johnson, Barbara Bates, Kathryn Garwood, Linda Nevalainen, Helen Olson, Ginger Shives, Wayne Simpson, Ken Conard, Jan Koets, Judy and Sarah Wilson, Rosemary Martin, Ginger, Gigi, Clint, and Patti Farmer.

Not everyone is bestowed with a personal poem created just for the occasion. Sincere gratitude to Fred Marler for 'The One Who Knows'.

Special appreciation goes to Pat Clankie who was proof-reader extraordinaire. She was extremely thorough, knowledgeable and gentle at the same time.

My dream was ultimately brought to fruition through the dedication and hard work of Casper Greyson (marketing), Bill Sanders (Publisher), Leslie (office coordinator) and all those involved with Tarbutton Press. They believed in Pawprints and gave it 'wings'.

Hugs all around to the animals featured in the book. They entered my life and live within me every hour of the day. I shall always be grateful for their love and the honor to have been a part of their lives.

PREFACE

It was just an ordinary day in suburbia—filled with a husband, children, cooking, cleaning, yard work, shopping, and paying bills—when the extraordinary happened. Our daughter came in the front door with a look of exhilaration on her face and a tumbling in her coat pocket. Out popped the bright-eyed face of a tiny kitten and my heart broke into a smile. This was a rather unique happening, for even though our Edgewood residence had long provided habitat to many animals, as we regularly care for our fair share of strays and vagabonds-- dogs, cats, tropical birds, squirrels and other assorted wildlife *critters*, this was the first *kitten* to ever enter our household. He simply glowed with the most vibrant orange coloring imaginable, and that little guy literally tugged away at the strings of my heart. At that very moment, he and I embarked on what was to become an exciting and galvanizing journey. No other name would fit him but 'Pumpkin'.

Pumpkin was only about the size of a handful of caramel popcorn—while being as vulnerable and helpless as a newborn baby. Smitten by his innocent appearance, it was impossible to get enough of his soft, airish-like fur, sweet innocence and radiant sparkle. For the next few days it seemed that every waking moment was centered on Pumpkin. He followed me and I followed him. We were rarely out of one another's sight.

Yes, my enchantment with him was extreme-- perhaps some would say an obsession, for I was bewitched by everything about him. I simply did not want to miss a single experience of his zestful exploration of life. He pranced, danced, wobbled, and hobbled--sparkled and shimmered like pure sunshine while imploring me to spend my day with him in play. Conceivably, the housework could have been done during his times of slumber, but that was when he looked his most enticing— so angelically pure that it was all but impossible to remove his oftentimes relaxed and slumbering body from its curled position in the crook of my arm. I was given at that time to understand the impulse of the prophet Mohammed who felt compelled to cut off the sleeve of his garment rather than to disturb the cat who had fallen asleep upon it.

Since none of the other animal lovers in our family or circle of friends even seemed to approach the realization of what a privilege it was just to be in the same room with Pumpkin, it seemed to me as if I alone was deserving of the honor to be the one whose life he had been assigned to share. Though I made countless efforts to illustrate his magnificence to others— my comments lacked the persuasion to unlock those necessary passageways in their hearts or to clear the obstacles that prevented them from sharing the glory which radiated from that glimmering orange heartthrob.

But is it even possible for any of us to actually enter the soul of another with our imaginings? Is it possible for one person to share what they perceive to be splendor and majesty with others? Surely it is so, for great artists, musicians, authors and orators have mastered that art for ages-- but how to share the simple wonders of a cat?

My inner emotions were rumbling and smoldering like a volcano about to erupt. Every fiber in my embodiment ached to translate my thoughts into words. I was all but bursting with over-ripe emotion. How I yearned to narrate his ermine touch, to transcend the power of his hypnotic control, and delve deep into the mystery of his cosmic energy.

Had I become consumed by my own zeal to inspire others to look beyond the kitten-cuteness and persuade them to acknowledge this profound celebrity that had now become one of us? Perhaps it was so, for on that warm October equinox, aglow in the background of golden and crimson leaves, that became my mission. I curled my trembling fingers around the cylinder of the nearest pen and began to write. The words spilled onto the page as my thoughts swirled like the white-water rapids of the mighty Colorado River. Verbs, adjectives, dangling participles spewing forth in a topsy-turvy blur as I grabbled for a foothold amid the pandemonium.

What a sensation of newly found joy and emotion had suddenly entered my life. There was a story to be told and every thread of my existence was searching for the ways to connect with those who shared similar interests. It was only to be a short story in narrative form and I titled it, "Everyone Should Own An Orange Cat." I wrote and wrote and wrote, but even after I had poured my heart onto paper and would have thought my task should be complete— there was still an unsettled voice within that could not be quelled. There were so many more stories to be told—and thus the birth of the book, *Pawprints Upon My Heart*.

For much of my life I had traveled a parallel path with what I perceived to be animal spirits and had always believed that all life forms are sacredly connected. Now the opportunity to place my emotions into words-- to explain those sensitive and heartfelt ties I had experienced with each individual creature of my past and present stood before me. I would now describe how those animal friends helped to create the person I have become. For you see, each of them left me with indelible memories. Every one of them left their pawprints upon my heart and it is therein that their loving remembrances will remain with me to the end.

Pawprints Upon My Heart is a progressive journey whose pathway is illuminated by a darling orange kitten that beckoned me to join him on a most wonderful adventure, and you are invited to accompany us. So welcome to our world-- our little Garden of Eden. But watch where you step for there are bunnies underfoot, birds overhead, cats napping in the sunshine and dogs playing tag around every bend.

EVERYONE SHOULD OWN
AN ORANGE CAT

A BLESSING CALLED PUMPKIN

Our family has always been surrounded by a multitude of animals. We usually had at least two dogs at the same time, sometimes three, and once (heaven forbid) four. Over the years, parakeets, cockatiels, and an Amazon parrot numbered among the furs and feathers that graced our halls and shredded our wallpaper. Once we had two sweet, supposedly female, Guinea pigs that surprised us with three little piglets and pet mice which multiplied so rapidly that a calculator would have been hard pressed to keep count.

After our children had flown from the nest, we settled down to the quiet normality of caring for ten pampered pets that included three king-sized housedogs, a trio of litter-trained bunnies and four cats. The cats were a pencil sketch of rescued orphans; gray and white, gray striped, pure black and lastly gray patched with white.

Feeding time at our home-zoo was a kaleidoscope of blacks, browns, and grays with a slight sprinkling of polka dots (our Dalmatian). I enjoyed their diversity in size and shape but the spectrum of color was a mundane blending of charcoal and muted hues.

AND THEN CAME PUMPKIN. He was a tiny male cast-off brought to us in the pocket of our daughter's coat... as fuzzy a kitten as ever I've seen and as bright orange as a county fair pumpkin. This little melon colored tiger-striped cub was soon to bring about a complete metamorphosis in our lives. Exactly how many times can you call your husband away from his computer to come see the new little kitten all snuggled up with a downy bunny or the great Halloween colors of two wrestling cats (black and orange) legs all entwined.

My husband was always politely amused by the spectacle and eventually began interrupting my chores when he spotted orange over gray, or a similar tangle of stripes sleeping together in the laundry basket.

Having this sweet marmalade kitten in our household was like seeing color for the first time. Adding this orange ribbon of color made the grays appear brighter, blacks took on shades of midnight, and browns glimmered with mahogany highlights. Pumpky made all of us aware of the harmony and contrast in every texture and perception of color in our lives. Sometimes Pumpkin would stroll through a ray of sunshine and I would gasp at the radiance he would emit. He actually glowed effervescent.

When the neighborhood kids would come to visit our 'petting zoo', they would inevitably ask if they could please take Pumpkin home with them. It was as though their hearts would break at the thought of releasing him from their embracing grasp. Even money bribes to acquire him were not uncommon and were offered in sincere confidence.

Right then and there I realized the magical effect this orange kitten had on young and old. His sunny brilliance lifted the spirits of all who met him. Something about Pumpkin caused man and beast to reach out to him and their reactions were identical. "This baby is special!"

Our house became known as 'Pumpkin's House' and sometimes, 'The Pumpkin Patch,' and we all seemed to grow brighter in his sunbeam. No animal ever felt over-shadowed or slighted by his popularity but just the opposite. We all smiled in unison when we witnessed him sprawled belly up on the couch or streaking full speed ahead like a bright golden comet.

Even my husband, at first an orange cat skeptic, amazed me at the power this kitten had over him. A spiritual man by nature, he jokingly informed me that if he were to precede me in death, he planned to return as a stray orange cat that would appear upon my doorstep. Nothing would be more heavenly to him than to be showered with the pure adoration the new foundling would experience. "Wish gladly granted," was my reply for then I would not only have two orange cats, but a feline guardian angel as well.

By now, I had come to the conclusion that everyone should own an orange cat. If the scientists who had cloned the sheep named Dolly had instead reproduced a bright tiger-striped kitten named Pumpkin, no negative comments or words of impending doom would have been uttered. This little ambassador of love, multiplied by the millions, would deliver more pure joy and inner peace than anything mankind could envision.

So... Prepare Ye the Way-- Open your heart-- Unburden your soul-- and accept the challenge of inviting an orange cat into your life.

PEDRO

OUR FINE FEATHERED FRIEND

Imagine being born in the wild, untamed jungles of South America. The thick, tangled growth of climbing vines weaving branch and leaf into a dense variegated green canopy high above the rain-forest floor. A never ceasing collage of animal voices; squalling birds, screeching monkeys, and chattering wildlife accentuated by a rainbow of vivid color-- royal purples, fiery reds, incandescent yellows and sapphire blues. The daily rainfall, extreme heat and drenching humidity generated the ideal environment for the birthplace and habitat of a magnificent species of bird known as the parrot. In the torrid tropics, everything, plant and animal, grows more vibrant and this perfect Shangri-La was likely the homeland of Pedro, our yellow-headed, Amazon parrot.

One can only speculate about the very early days of Pedro's life. Documentary exposes have filmed multitudes of young parrots being smuggled out of their jungle paradise and the shameful atrocities they endured. Tightly packed into crates and cages with no regard for life except to ensure the optimal cash crop, many young birds perish during transport. Those surviving face an uncertain future at the hands of merciless contraband brokers. Pet stores, parrot dealers, or black-market criminals, at this point, just the luck (or bad luck) of the draw determines the fate of these bewildered new immigrants.

Pedro was likely one of the many legal birds

brought to the States, but the procurement of parrots is the same either way. These helpless creatures find themselves snatched from a feather-lined nest and victims of a frantic, traumatic kidnapping. The once tranquil and peaceful air is shattered by their mother's heartbroken and helpless calls mingled with the fearful cries from terrified babies being roughly seized and separated from the only maternal love they would have ever known. Then spirited away to the U.S. and other ports, their beloved freedom is gone forever and the lush jungle becoming only a faded memory. Waiting ahead was a future as unsettling and confusing as the bizarre new surroundings.

Whatever harrowing and agonizing events that had occurred to young Pedro were now in the past, his destination was America and a pet store encased in concrete and stone. He was housed in a barred enclosure with two other tropical birds. Everything appeared foreign to him-- harsh artificial lighting, unfamiliar cage mates, noisy human voices attached to groping hands and even the food was tastelessly bland. Still, this infant bird had a jungle survival spirit and tried his best to acclimate to his new domain but even his best attempts to fit in or adjust were short lived and quickly squelched.

All of us have experienced playground bullies. They have likely been around since the beginning of swings and slides. Their skills of intimidation and instilling fear are legendary and those of us who were mercifully spared from their venom were not untouched by the scars that we witnessed seared onto their hapless victims. The human characteristics attributed to the classic bully-- cruelty, oppression, tormenting and physical punishment can be found in many species in nature and the two cellmates in the pet shop aviary were poised and waiting for their unsuspecting target.

Pedro was but a young bird taken too early from his

mother to understand things like group behavior controlled by a social system of dominance and subordination. Nor was he one of those advertised hand-fed baby birds that are so pliable, trainable and lovable. He was never caressed and nurtured by an experienced bird trainer but simply plucked from the nest and thrust into hostile territory ruled by two tyrannical comrades not at all interested in welcoming the new inmate. Their brutish size intimidated him and his apprehension fueled their aggression. Puncturing bites and threatening body language continually frightened him from the food and water bowl. Sleep was impossible with the enemy just inches away and the engulfing terror caused by frequent assaults found Pedro cowering at the bottom of the cage.

A Good Samaritan, perhaps divinely led to this pet store, witnessed the brutality endured by the new baby parrot. She alerted the clerk to the intolerable situation but her concerns were disregarded as insignificant and she was assured that 'they would learn to get along'. Suffering through anguishing days and nights filled with paralyzing fear, the life began to ebb from the tiny bird. The concerned humanitarian, her happiness and contentment jeopardized by this heart-rending drama felt compelled to intervene. Working as a clerk and living on a meager salary, she unselfishly sacrificed an entire paycheck to rescue this withdrawn, shivering creature huddled in the far corner of his minute prison. This wonderful lady could truly be titled an unsung hero.

"Free at last, free at last, thank God-Almighty, I'm free at last." The baby parrot thanked her with his grateful gaze and immediately fell into a deep sound sleep, perhaps the first safe slumber he had experienced since that raid in the jungle. His confinement was still a cage, but sheltered and secure… a haven… his home.

This deed was not done to procure a prized material

possession but simply to put an end to the tribulation of this young innocent. The buyer had never intended to keep her costly purchase but went straight away to the small photography studio of a mutual friend. Pleading her case and the plight of this anxiety filled orphan, the freelance photographer was easily persuaded to keep the valuable gift and graciously promised to rehabilitate and restore the confidence of this trauma-damaged soul.

Fate had mercifully intervened and Pedro had a new home. He was now the center of attention. This colorfully plumed misfit soon became the office mascot. His cage straddled the reception desk and while greeting all customers he reveled in the adoring attention. A quick study, he soon developed a vocabulary and delighted all who came to visit him. Life was good and he felt content-- this little frightened bird who was suddenly important seemed to sense that he had become a novelty... a precious jewel.

As we all know, life can be cruel or kind and a life span of a caged animal can range from sadly short to antagonistically long. An Amazon parrot and most large tropical birds can live up to fifty-five years and depending on their care, the time span could be a blessing or a curse. Being creatures of the treetops and lofty heights, just existing in confinement might break the spirit of many a bird, but consideration and attention from a kind, caring owner can enhance the quality of their prolonged life.

After two years, the photographer joined a larger, established studio and Pedro was relocated to his home. His world changed completely. He now had a family consisting of the photographer, his wife and their twin college-aged sons. Pedro listened to music for the first time, sat in the window and basked in the sunshine. He was occasionally allowed to fly and was mesmerized by that noisy invention called television. This house was alive with animals and it was no time at all until he became a pet himself. The sounds that surrounded him had changed from office chatter to the daily interactions between family members, their pets and friends. Pedro learned to sing (in an operatic style vibrato), imitate cat-purring sounds and could call each occupant of the house by name. He memorized everyone's routine, their voices and habits while eagerly watching the seasons of time march on. Pedro lived five years in that house and assumed that the permanence of his daily routine was much like the perpetual rising and setting of the sun.

But life at best is a journey beset with rocky crevices and sometimes people begin to drop out of step with one another, grow apart, and fall into those craggy pits. A cold, icy chill had come over this once ideal family and the existence that Pedro had grown accustomed to began to mutate. Happiness and laughter were replaced with upheaval, stress, crying and silence. Cheerful voices were no longer heard. Anger unnerved marital harmony and formally loved pets were ignored and forgotten.

Pedro's cage was moved to a windowless, desolate area of the photographer's dark room and covered with plastic to keep his 'messiness' inside. The daily cleaning of his cage was abandoned and his waste soon piled up to the bottom of his perch. Feeding was sporadic and minimal, limited only to an occasional handful of seeds as all fruit or vegetable treats were terminated and long forgotten. The wife had been the caregiver for the past years but now she had moved away and the necessary care for a faithful pet was too large an obstacle for the anxiety-filled photographer to cope with.

The photographer did not intentionally cause Pedro's emotional and physical decline, but due to his depression, acts of apathy and neglect became the norm.

Both Pedro's health and mental stability became another casualty in this human's personal war.

So there he waited, enclosed in his opaque rectangle, yearning for a kind voice or a caring gesture. Pedro was disheveled and no longer sang or spoke. He had become a zombie catacombed in a perpetual bog of the living dead.

Two years went by. Then one Sunday morning a call awoke us from our slumber. "Mary, Ben... would you take Pedro?" No explanation, just the voice of one who was so mired in melancholy that even asking the question drained his strength. I was speechless-- another animal-- but an affirmative nod from my sleepy husband confirmed both of our feelings. "Absolutely. Bring him right over."

We waited with bated breath that this was really happening, that he wouldn't change his mind at the last minute. We felt like we were rescuing a sadly abused child from a filthy tenement flat and when he was safely in our custody, we rejoiced. He was grungy, a musty odor permeated his feathers and we relished tearing off his obscure cover and exposing him to the daylight. We washed and scrubbed his cage while spritzing him with warm water. After the dirty droplets had fallen off him we finished his cleanup by blow-drying his feathers until they were soft and downy.

Next on the agenda was nutrition. Banana slices, lettuce, green beans, carrots, and grapes-- true manna from the gods-- overflowed his food bowl. Nothing was withheld, every bite savored. Senses that had been dulled awakened from a coma-like state and Pedro began to observe his new surroundings. He was like a little flower bud opening a tiny bit more each day. Long forgotten habits slowly came back. Once again he was attentively listening to the sounds around him, singing, talking and even flying. All these activities would eventually return him to the bird he used to be.

Of course life wouldn't seem like a soap opera without the impending doom scene. It began one morning when to our horror we received an unexpected phone call from the photographer. He first asked and then demanded Pedro back. Seems he had a new girlfriend and wanted to impress her with an unusual gift. PEDRO!!! I now understood how defiant a mother bear feels when her cub is in danger. An emotional outrage fueled by anger assaulted me and the resulting primal response became that of protector. Diplomacy was my initial approach to him. I described how Pedro had become a part of our family, was adjusting wonderfully and how we adored him. I franticly rambled on about the new colors that were coming back to his feathers, his obvious happiness and renewed health. All I had said was in vain. My words were falling on deaf ears and an unyielding, cold heart. He insisted I return his 'property' to him immediately. After about thirty minutes of this escalating tirade, I simply stated, "No. He is ours now and you are not getting him back."

The conversation drained me. I was shaking and felt nauseous. He had accused, fumed, and threatened, completely oblivious to the tender feelings that he was cruelly trampling on. The entire scenario had become very ugly and a scene foreign to this longtime friendship. Yet, we were not going to return that bird to anyone, friend or foe, with such a track record of neglect to abuse again. Our newly assigned and accepted position as gatekeeper to Pedro's cage was secure. We were dedicated to defending his self-esteem and safeguarding his new refuge. We won both the battle and the war.

Pedro remained with us and after a time the photographer apologized for his former misdeed. His romance had been short-lived and if we had conceded to his temporarily impaired reasoning, Pedro would have been lost to us forever.

Pedro has now been with us for fifteen years and his dignity as well as confidence is completely restored. Healthy, noisy, interacting with cats and humans, he has found a place of his own. His future is solid and our children have promised to continue to care for him if anything should happen to us. They know his history and feel obligated to the guarantee we assured him.

During the summer months he rules the roost outside. We place his cage on our deck during the day as he fills the air with his singing and constant gibbering giving a command performance to all that seek him out-- a natural born ham. He likely has a long life ahead of him, years and years of memories, and we dearly hope all of them will be good ones.

Live long and care free Pedro. We are proud to call you friend.

WHAT CAN I SAY?

HIS NAME IS DEXTER.

The story of Dexter is a paradox of highs and lows, joys and sorrow, confusion and trust. As I sit here deep in thought recalling the events that shaped his life and personality, I observe him tightly snuggled against the bodies of our German shorthaired pointer, Rowdy, and Doberman, Bubba. I take great pleasure when I catch a glimpse of the serenely peaceful expression on Dexter's face. It wasn't always so.

His name is Dexter and our daughter, Gigi, chose him to fill a very large void in her heart. Raised all of her life in a home over-flowing with animals, when she made the move to living single she also faced the circumstance of being pet-less. As the years progressed, she was haunted by a deep-seated loneliness and longing for the companionship only offered by a faithful, four-footed friend. The solution to her dilemma was obvious, but being committed to teaching grade school, aerobics classes and sport activities, she wisely decided that summer break would be the ideal time for her to adopt the perfect puppy.

It would be amiss not to mention the fact that as her parents we cautioned her time after time against making this life-changing decision. She lived in a vast condo complex, on the fourth floor no less, and was a very actively involved individual… often away from home. But Gigi, being much like her pet addicted parents, threw caution to the wind by following her heart and purchased a delightfully friendly Dalmatian puppy.

His arrival was actually a well-kept secret from us for a while, as evidently she did not want even one dark cloud to infringe upon the indelible bond between her and this enchanting new baby. No disheartening phrases like "We told you so," or "You'll be sorry," often used to predict impending doom were to be tolerated at this momentous junction in her life.

So, for all that endless, sun filled summer Gigi and Dexter were inseparable. They were off to volleyball games, burgers at McDonald's, car rides just to be together, long runs on the ski-hill and daily walks through the wooded terrain that surrounded her building. The days were long, hot and glorious and their affection for one another was apparent to everyone who observed them always together. Gigi and Dexter slept side-by-side in her bed, shared every hour of the day and he trusted this idyllic life would last forever.

Alas, summer vacation ended all too soon, as every teacher can tell you, and the start of the new school term had arrived. The change in their lifestyle was dramatic; starting with the shattering early morning alarm followed by a flurry of activity and then complete solitude... hour after hour... day after day. Dexter was stunned, numb and confused by the sudden bleakness of his existence. Nothing in his reasoning capacity could explain what had possibly gone wrong.

He had been the absolute darling of the complex; funny, endearing, 'Mr. Personality Plus' to all who met him and now he felt abandoned, rejected and worst of all... completely alone. He tried to fill the long, dull, aching hours with sleep but this young pup had spent his days running or exploring the walking trails and it was foreign to his nature not to be on the go.

With all this time on his paws, Dexter began, as

they say in school lingo, to act out. Likely the combination of many emotions ruled his actions-- boredom, temper, or maybe just a craving for some fun. The apartment became his own personal playground and nothing was considered out of bounds. Best of all, he now made all the rules. Being selective of his playthings enhanced much of the adventure. Chew bones and boring dog toys were soon ignored and row upon row of neatly lined shoes left exposed by a partially ajar closet door smelled intriguing. One shoe from each pair, now that was a creative playtime activity as he suddenly realized being alone could be fun if he used a little imagination.

Next came purses and their contents-- wallets, brushes, glasses and even her credit cards (except in this particular case the credit card mutilation was a mixed blessing). Everything became the victim of puppy tooth-prints.

When our weary schoolteacher finally arrived home, eager for the solace of her castle, imagine the tornado of emotions as she opened that door. There stood Dexter-- ecstatic with joy upon seeing her and beaming from ear to ear with pride at all the chaos he had created. Hadn't he been a busy boy?

Instead of the loving embrace and baby talk he had expected, a barrage of angry tones mixed with utter despair shattered his jubilation. He had longed for her all day. Even when he was busy demolishing shoes, it was her scent that inspired him. And now, no reward, no praise, but something he had never experienced before-- disappointment and scorn. His illusions were shattered; the anticipated homecoming became a terrible nightmare that he just could not seem to wake up from.

Only Gigi and Dexter know what happened next. Maybe there was a first spanking or possibly just harsh words but positively there were tears of anguish shed by both. The seeds of resentment and anxiety had been sown as each role in this drama was clearly defined. Dexter became the misbehaving, naughty child punishing the sole parent for not understanding his unhappiness. He was the pampered baby suddenly snatched from his mother's loving arms and abandoned in a prison-like daycare suffering from separation anxiety in solitary confinement. Perhaps in his restricted capacity to reason, he determined that if he was bad enough she would not leave him again and things would return to the companion-filled days of yore.

Gigi became the bedraggled single parent working long, exhausting hours to pay the ever-mounting bills that supplied their needs. Each day upon returning home, she realized she might be facing new financial loss and was often disheartened as she painfully surveyed the continuing disasters. She, like Dexter, longed for those carefree days of summer that they had previously shared, but the present reality was that the flame between them was cooling fast. Closet doors were firmly latched and chewable valuables were placed beyond his reach, but just as old problems were resolved new ones developed.

Even a potty-trained puppy realizes that eight hours is an impossible task of self-control. Pushed beyond endurance, well-learned habits are soon abandoned. These accidents were never malicious, just the call of nature, but nevertheless the results were damaging, expensive, and permanent. The solution seemed to be restriction of daytime water, a sunrise jogging session and a reassuring concentration of loving affection.

The situation improved for a while but sadly the tranquility was short lived. The early morning run was over too soon, the fall weather delightfully mild, and the laughter so joyful that Dexter decided he no longer wanted to return to the confinement of the apartment and the long lonely day ahead.

Taking advantage of not being on a leash, he made a frantic break for freedom. No amount of calling, bribing, cajoling, or threatening tones could convince him to relinquish his newfound heavenly pursuit. A desperately late employee watchful of the passing minutes while dreading the reality of a classroom filled with mischievous second graders brought the crisis to the breaking point. When finally captured, punishment was the frustrated reaction.

Sadly this daily repetition became the norm in their morning ritual. So now, even his once lovingly spoken, beloved name –Dexter-- meant that he was in trouble and this boy definitely did not like trouble. Sigmund Freud could have written a chapter on the cause and effect of turmoil featuring these two characters.

Dexter had become a dog with an unpredictable potty problem— a dog that would no longer respond to his name— a dog that could not be trusted with personal possessions— a dog that had developed an attitude of defiant rebellion. One can only imagine how this schoolteacher would have felt about a parent of such a child, but in this helpless case she was the mom.

Every course of action was only a temporary solution, as bad habits were never totally corrected and good habits were soon forgotten. Things got progressively worse. Frustrated neighbors were now complaining about the constant daytime yowling and monetary fines by the building management for misdeeds were levied upon the strained household budget. A relationship once built on love and trust was crumbling under the strain. It was like a house of cards that had come tumbling down when we received that dreaded yet inevitable phone call.

"Mom and Dad... I can't keep Dexter. Can you help

me find a good home for him?" Gigi cried when she said it and it broke our hearts to hear it, but the decree was set in stone and the deed was already in motion. There were no chastising phrases-- only gentle compassion for the wrenching pain both souls, human and canine, were experiencing.

A phone call to some country friends helped us contact a horse-breeding family that found a new home for Dexter. The very next day we drove the seventy miles to Gigi's apartment and transported Dexter along with his belongings off to a new life. He was thrilled to see us, and yes, we stopped at McDonald's for a treat while enjoying his good nature and loving attention during the hour-long ride.

A charming home in the countryside with a retired caregiver in her early 70's was to be Dexter's destiny. There was an immediate mutual attraction between them and when we left he seemed quite content to stay with a new mom who assured us he would have the best life a pampered pooch could want. Over the next three months we kept in touch with Dexter's new owner. His adjustment was phenomenal, but then one day out of the blue, we received a phone call stating she was moving, and could no longer keep him. Would we take him back?

We went to retrieve him and assured her that all was fine. We completely understood and fully appreciated the caregiving contributions she had already made. But in reality, we were in shock and consumed with apprehension. After all, our household was now bursting at the seams with seventeen in-house animals and we had finally achieved perfect harmony in our blended animal family. Everyone got along great-- no fighting or stress-- just complete acceptance and heavenly peacefulness. Enter... Cousin Dexter.

This little polka-dotted, ever-so-pampered pup had

ballooned into the dog version of a 'sumo-wrestler'. Three months of yummy snacks galore and being fed on demand had transformed Dexter into a Dalmatian shaped like a mother sow. His physique went straight back from massive shoulders into a bulging belly followed by a bulbous butt. He looked like a huge porker-dotted marshmallow and felt like a foam rubber pillow. But was he happy to see us!

We hauled him back to our house and that's when all havoc broke loose. He barged through the front door-- wildly leaped onto the family room couch-- vaulted over to Ben's favorite chair-- wiped out the floral centerpiece on the coffee table and barreled off toward the kitchen. Every animal food dish was licked clean in a matter of seconds. Water bowls were slurped bone dry, and two spotted front feet on the countertop positioned the jaws of destruction dangerously close to a gigantic bowl of chips. Enough food to feed an army disappeared down his throat without the privilege of even being chewed. The entire household-- dogs, cats, people, bunnies, parrot, all staring in disbelief-- mouths agape in unison. Peck's bad boy was on the premises and civilized life as we had once known it was spinning out of control. Our perfect little animal paradise had been plummeted into Dante's inferno in the time span of a few short minutes.

Remember my spiritual husband? Well, he wasn't feeling too divinely inspired during all this *unheavenly* upheaval. We felt obligated to Dexter, but knew we couldn't keep him, so we took on the challenge of finding him another good home.

My husband, a devout man of lists, labored to compose one for the new prospective owners and with that mindset developed the necessary ground rules. 1. Dexter must be allowed on the couch. 2. He needs to sleep in their bed. 3. No chaining outside in the chilly weather (Dexter hates the cold and has absolutely no use for rain either). 4. Should have company home with him all day-- he gets lonely. 5. Likes McDonald's hamburgers (a lot!) 6. Must have a fenced-in yard. Get the gist of the list? Interested people read the requirements and just smiled while commenting, "My spouse should be treated so well."

Days, weeks, then months passed. He was always on the run, could not settle down, and his behavior was extremely hyperactive. Rugs, animals, and people were flung in startled disarray whenever he plowed by. Dexter could never quite maneuver around us without giving our knees a whack and we experienced cold-blooded terror whenever we met him midway on the stairs. The tranquil atmosphere of the household was now aboil with feline hissing, spitting and guttural sounds that sent hair-raising chills down our spines. We were hoarse from yelling, our cats were traumatized but Bubba and Rowdy thought it was great. This was the most fun they ever had in the house with Dexter leading them on wild races through the halls, roughhousing in the living room, and chasing hysterical cats at every opportunity. Boy, Cousin Dexter sure knew how to have a good time.

We were hollow eyed, just waiting for the next disaster-- nerves on edge when Dexter finally caught on to the rhythms of his new environment and began to settle down. He loved our fenced in yard and the freedom to wander wherever he pleased. It seemed all he ever wanted was a place to call his own and soon every nook and cranny was claimed as his personal treasure. Dexter could now run and play with the dogs, and was learning to tolerate the cats. Little by little, he matured into quite the composed gentleman. He was assigned a couch in an exposed-basement and was never required to linger outside in the cold or rain. He had a stay-at-home mother and now and then one of his beloved McDonald's hamburgers. Without so intending, we seemingly had passed all the requirements to become the permanent owners of Dexter dog.

But the best times of all were when Gigi came home for a visit. The two of them, now stress and obligation free could once again love and enjoy one another. They communicated in their own language and any bad memories of their past had long faded away. Gigi now realized that Dexter was being cared for and was grateful that she could still be a small part of his life.

UPDATE:

Fairy tale endings. Are they only possible in the lives of Cinderella and Sleeping Beauty, or can a perfect finale actually happen to people and animals in the here and now? Well, if you ask Dexter, he will tell you it is okay to believe in happy endings— for sometimes, good things do happen to Dexter dogs. For you see— came the day when Gigi married her Prince Charming, 'Chad'. The fact that Chad already had someone special in his life named C.D. [Chad's dog]--and a Bassett Hound of all things, let her know that animals would always be an important part of their equation. Upon their marriage, the combining of her four cats and his one dog would not have seemed quite complete without the most wonderful reunion of returning Dexter to the first love of his life. Back in the arms of Gigi, he was the hunter finally home from the hunt and the sailor home from the sea.

Now Dexter had both a Mom and a Dad, a quartet of cats to chase and a new low-rider pal to romp and roughhouse with. The fairy tale life with the King, Queen, and loyal entourage of four-legged subjects appeared quite perfect. Yet, there was still some fairy dust waiting to be sprinkled. A surprise was looming on the horizon and arrived with great fanfare following a rollercoaster pregnancy.

Presenting: Taa-ta-ta-taa, the Princesses! Yes, two identical twin girls christened with the titles of Princess Heather and Princess Tiffany. The kingdom was now bursting with activity as Chad, Gigi, Heather, Tiffany, Dexter, C.D., Sushie, Simba, Jigger, and little Einstein cat can go forth together.

Could anyone have possibly envisioned an ending so delightful and magical? Perhaps... but could it be that Dexter may have known the power of wishing upon those twinkling stars? How would he have planned it? What words could possibly have set all the pieces of this puzzle so perfectly into place? Perchance it was accomplished by simply wishing "to live happily ever after."

BERNIE AND GRAY CAT

A MIDSUMMER-NIGHT'S DREAM

My favorite subculture of the human race happens to be those persons who are dedicated animal lovers. Some, like us, may seem strangely odd with their obsessive compulsion to bring pet trivia into every conversation and the mushy gush that flows from their mouths concerning their darling sweeties knows no bounds of embarrassment. Our eyes tend to glaze over into a dazzling sparkle whenever recalling entertaining anecdotes and tears well up when reminiscing about pets long departed. Personally, I delight in being part of that flock and find myself dividing the general populace into those who love animals and those who don't.

So, it is no wonder at my amusement each and every time I share the fact I am writing a book based on the chronicles and adventures of the many animal spirits which have brightened our lives, I am often taken aside to hear a remarkable story the teller feels must be translated into print. From neighbors and friends to almost complete strangers, the sharing of animal friendship is a universal pleasure and I marvel at the devoted affection and touching sensitivity conveyed in their tales.

This story begins with our next-door neighbor, Barbara, and the Shakespearean drama that enlightened her life last summer. Barbara's household is a day and night contrast from ours. Whereas we are the neighborhood's 'Noah's Ark' with our endless variety of feline, canine and fowl, she has opted for the sedate lifestyle of a single, genteel cat as her companion of choice. An exclusive relationship, free of distractions from a husband or children no longer living at home, her interests centered on the demands and needs of an 'only' cat. Barbara's life was highlighted by quiet, calm and complacent evenings in front of the fireplace with just the two of them serenely sitting side by side in perfect harmony.

Barbara's soul mates have always been male cats descended from purebred and pedigreed ancestors. The first compatriot was named Dean, a grandiose Cameo Persian as stately and dignified as the lord of the manor should be. His long, pampered life ended peacefully and painlessly after seventeen treasured years together. The next cherished darling invited onto her lap was named Silver, an exquisitely handsome shaded silver Persian, not at all like his predecessor but a charming, loving individual in his own way. He was an exotic looking beauty, quick and nimble of foot, who gave Barbara seven years of special remembrances. He too passed on into the great unknown leaving a tremendous gaping chasm in her grieving, anguished heart.

After the loss of Silver, Barbara could not entertain the thought of ever replacing him. The death of so dear a friend and having to bury another favorite in her garden was more than she could face. The decision to avoid this pain was made. There would be no successor to Silver. That being the case, she would remain alone and lonely (?) for the rest of her life and so the once cheery house abundant with splendid memories became drearily morose where nothing remained but the sad stillness of a solitary occupant. No efforts from well-meaning and frequently visiting friends could invade the darkness or deter her melancholy emotional departure from life.

Then an opportunity for a European holiday was placed at her feet and an invisible nudging force encouraged the partaking of the trip. Her spirit was not in a traveling mood but she felt helpless to try to stop the chain of events and found herself half-heartedly jetting off to sunny Italy. Stepping off onto this foreign soil she was immediately overwhelmed by the eminence of this historically ancient and legendary ageless land. Barbara was awestruck by the celestial energy radiating from the opulent Renaissance architecture and vast abundance of world famous artwork found throughout Italy. This was the birthplace of immortal and timeless Latin literature saturated in the influence of Greek Mythology and the very origin of culture. The enchantment of this little boot-shaped peninsula bathed in the sky blue Mediterranean and Adriatic seas coursed through her veins and exchanged dull pain into sheer joy. She felt re-born, alive once again as no sorrow could survive in the presence of the acknowledged excellence of the great masters: Leonardo da Vinci, Raphael, Michelangelo, Donatello, Rossini, and Verdi. To actually stand in the sacred presence of these masterpieces had a miraculous effect on this emotionally numb traveler. As she translated the meaning of each of their works of art and drank in the glory of their accomplishments the spark that had fueled their lives rekindled her extinguished candle, which had been doused by sadness and grief.

The transfusion had begun and a day trip to Verona was the summit of her entire vacation. This was the sacred ground that so influenced William Shakespeare; the air still filled with the ambiance of his spirit. The atmosphere was electric-- bustling open-air markets filled with wondrous sights and smells. The magnificent ancient amphitheater there had been used as the background for the staging for many of his infamous dramas and comedies. It was here; amid all this magic and grandeur that Barbara had her vision. Her traumatized heart had been healed, shaken faith restored and the illumination had come back into cheerless eyes. She had been gifted with the meaning of life. Simply stated, we were placed here on earth to experience love and God's most precious presents to us were those beings from the animal kingdom. Yes, she was ready to bring another cat into her world. She would dare to unloose her heartstrings and relish the tender, gentle feelings that she had been denying.

She returned home from Italy a changed person. There was a visible vitality in her demeanor, a spring in her step, and a determined look upon her face. Days and evenings would no longer be secluded or isolated for she was to have that intended kitten. This time Barbara decided on a male Ragdoll, a breed characterized for its tremendous size and affectionate temperament. She called him Bernardo in honor of a character portrayed in a Shakespearean drama but shortened it to Bernie to better fit the tiny, boundless bundle of energy that she had chosen to share her life with.

Bernie had been born in a household brimming with noisy jubilation. He was just a tiny piece in the busy maze of a family crawling with children, cats, and dogs all entangled with toys, shoes, and household clutter. A never-ending flurry of activity and surplus of playful fun surrounded him. He had been one of many and when he left there with his new mom, Barbara, he crossed the threshold into a different culture and a brand new universe.

Bernie found himself one teeny kitten alone in a huge house; picture perfect, neatly decorated and soothingly silent. Barbara was there of course showering him with little kisses, caresses and all the love any pet could ever desire, but Bernie had come from hustling Grand Central Station and now was in the awesome

Vatican-like presence of an antique filled house. There was so much to explore, so much to learn as they began to blend their lives together. Everyday Barbara and Bernie discovered something new about each other, a world of infinite surprises and little by little they wove a beautiful tapestry of life together.

Spring came gracefully that year as windows and patio doors were flung open to the delight of the winter weary housebound occupants. At first Bernie was cautious about venturing out onto the second story wooden deck into the soft, moist breeze, but the intoxicating smells wafted over him and he was soon a frequent fixture on his favorite observation post. Endless hours were spent in sweet repose in the soft shade of the huge towering oaks that surrounded his tree house.

Hark! Hark! The wind of change was in the air for the unsuspecting Bernie. The afternoon of this fateful day was similar to all others that had passed that spring. A sprawled out Bernie basking in a sliver of sunshine, limply lying like the rag doll he was, tiny slits of eyes barely capable of focusing, caught the slightest movement of a sultry shadow among the bursting green sprouts in the garden below. A faint breeze delivered a provocative scent to his twitching nose causing curiosity to elevate his head ever so slightly.

A delicate white foot cautiously appeared out from under a bush, then a long sleek leg, stealth and deliberately placed into his range of vision. Like an enchanted fairy that has allowed herself to be discovered, this gazelle like beauty emerged from the shady cover to stand in full view of the breathless Bernie. It was a vision of loveliness that his eyes were drinking in, a spell binding apparition... the Venus de Milo, perfection extraordinaire. The white of the legs contrasted with the downy gray that clothed the rest of this heavenly body and that angelic face, which gently lifted upward ever so slightly toward the anxious admirer, was the most flawless image this male had ever witnessed. A face trimmed in gray fur with a perfect triangle of white accenting almond-shaped green eyes lined with silky black lashes and a pedal of gray color surrounding the delicate, sooty black nose.

Mere words could not possibly describe the preeminence he had discovered in his own backyard and the heightened emotion that he was feeling from his cupid arrowed heart. Eyes locked in amorous admiration, Bernie and Gray cat, had surrendered their souls to one another.

Yes, the love bug had bitten Bernie. This was the first and only cat that he had seen in many months for all his memories of littermates had disappeared in the fog of youth. He had quite honestly forgotten what another cat looked like and seeing 'her' was like visiting a foreign planet and suddenly coming face to face with another of your species. The thrill electrified his mind.

William Shakespeare had set the stage for this scene hundreds of years ago. The balcony lover hailed by the clandestine garden visitor, two star-crossed participants from blatantly different backgrounds. The Shakespearean characters were Romeo and Juliet; a male and female of the human persuasion but this play featured different actors under similarly distressing circumstances. The emotions and urgency of their plight was just as severely intense as the famous playwright had conjured.

You see, Gray cat was slowly starving to death. She had been tossed out, discarded, abandoned by an owner she had trusted and loved. This ghastly deed had been done in haste for these immoral villains who deserted her did not want to be caught in this deplorable crime. Committed under the blanket of night, their betrayal was evident in the car's abrupt stop and then screeching retreat. Gray cat was cruelly left helplessly disoriented sitting on the barren cement curb in a strange, alien neighborhood. They never once glanced back and saw her frightened eyes nor cared if she died from the gnawing pain of malnutrition, slowly wasting away from disease or became the bloody, mauled victim of a vicious dog. She was less than garbage to them, this dainty, vulnerable, loving pet that had given her loyalty and devotion simply for a touch of their hand.

Just one of the millions of throw away pets-- pampered and doted on as a kitten but deplored when she became an adult cat. Gray cat had no survival instincts, as they never developed in one who had only known a full supper bowl and soft blanket to curl up in.

All she could do was wander aimlessly looking for something familiar while desperately searching for a comforting smell that reminded her of home. Dense bushes with muddy underbrush tangled her fur and dirtied her face. She knew nothing of hunting, for her mice had been toys used to entice her to play. Every small animal scurried away at the mere sight of her and the birds sounded a frantic warning whenever she was near. Hunger forced her to eat grass but that eventually was vomited up leaving her weakened and trembling in pain. Nighttime surrounded her and the nocturnal creatures that slunk out of the shadows were even more frightful than she could have imagined. Snarling raccoons fighting over a scrap of food shattered the blackness and all she could do was huddle deeper into the gnarly center of an evergreen hoping they would not notice her shaking body. Her mind swirled with questions-- where was she? What was happening to her? Had she done something to bring about this doom?

The days and nights became a jangled maze. No

one wanted her around. People angrily shooed her away from their bird feeders and neighborhood boys became assailants with rakes and shovels laughing at her fearful reaction. Gray cat had tried to get close to the human strangers but was expelled from yards and garages as though she were a thieving vagabond or a pestilence threatening their complacent world.

No one saw the lost soul in search of a tiny shred of compassion or just one random act of kindness but instead viewed her as a chipmunk killer, a molester of birds, a leper in her own animal kingdom. Starving, thirsty, bone tired and broken spirited she just gave up. This tormented victim succumbed to defeat and lay down to die in a quiet garden when she attempted one last desperate act and showed herself to the elegant, lofty presence reclining on the high wooden deck. Perhaps he would help her and take pity on this scruffy, skeleton of a cat. Her eyes pleaded her case, "Please help me. I have no one who cares that I am frightened, hungry and scorned by mankind. My death is imminent."

The message was relayed from the homeless waif and received by the lion hearted recipient. Bernardo knew his destiny. There was a damsel in distress who needed him and he alone was responsible for saving her. "O Romeo, Romeo, Wherefore art thou Romeo?" There he was on his balcony, only this time his name was Bernie and through their telepathic communication he sensed that he had been chosen to reverse the downward spiral her life was taking.

From that day forward Barbara's placid, peaceful household was never the same. Bernie, the quiet and calm homeboy that Barbara had loved so well transformed into the most obnoxious, noisy bundle of neuroses in the history of cats. He was on a mission and giving it all that he was worth. He began by pacing from window to window then door to door, yowling and howling at the tip-top volume of his lungs. His singing cantor was uneven and decidedly off key creating the searing effect of fingernails scratching on a blackboard. Once he started, no one could stop him from his obsessive ritual and the words incessant, unnerving, and noise pollution described him to a tee. Nothing would appease him. No sweet talk or tasty treats would sway him away from the windows or cause him to cease his endless racket.

At first Barbara was amused by his antics-- just a little idiosyncrasy in her wonderful cat. But as the hours, days, and weeks wore on the volume increased to ear shattering levels and she didn't think it was quite so cute. When he finally did take a breather, Barbara would fall into a fitful sleep only to be jolted back into reality by Bernie at five AM at the foot of her bed verbalizing his unhappiness in deafening tones.

Barbara began to crumble from all the noise, hyper-action, and stress. Was it possible her cat was mentally deranged? She consulted everyone for advice on what could cause this Dr. Jekyll and Mr. Hyde behavior in her gorgeous, otherwise well-behaved Bernie. No one had any answers or had even heard of anything so bizarre. A solution to this disastrous predicament had to be forthright or little Bernie would have to be taken in for some professional help.

Finally Barbara could take no more. It had been hours since he had started before dawn and no human being was capable of withstanding the continued torment. She dragged herself outside to the solace of her garden and wearily slumped into her lawn chair. As her frazzled nervous system began to calm she realized that a tiny face with a beckoning expression was watching her every move.

It was a cat. A painfully thin, nasty looking stray with dull, gray, filthy white fur that had matted so badly it hung in huge clumps bunched around its neck followed by a tail that seemed to be stuck permanently down by a sappy residue. There it sat among the pink impatiens and delicate woodland wildflowers, a tattered ragamuffin in contrast to their splendid glory. Weakened from hunger and frail from lack of care, it no longer had the strength to approach a human but neither did it have the desire to run away. A sight tragically pathetic to see, Barbara's soft and sympathetic heart immediately reacted with compassion and benevolence. How ironic that inside her house was her expensive illustrious cat misbehaving badly and outside was this bedraggled, little tramp ever so gently asking for a hand out.

A bowl of cat food was quickly produced and the famished victim of circumstance wolfed down the life sustaining contents. Upon finishing every morsel, Gray cat gave an indebted glance and then abruptly disappeared back into the undergrowth. Barbara returned inside to wash the bowl and was stunned by the tomb-like silence that greeted her. Had Bernie had a heart attack and died? No, he was busy finishing off his supper and heading for his favorite sleeping place on the couch. Dr. Jekyll (or the good Bernie) was back. Hallelujah! Time for rejoicing by taking a sorely needed nap.

Oh Glorious Day! Her juvenile delinquent seemed repentant and perhaps all previous troubles were solved. Bernie was docile for the entire day and Barbara had forgiven him all his transgressions. That was until five A.M when Bernie pounced on her with added zest. Yowl, howl, bawl, and then a dash to the window.... over and over and over again. Barbara walked over to where Bernie's fixed and rigid body was pressed against the pane. What was his problem? And there it was-- Gray cat, sitting statue-like and still, just peering in at her and Bernie. Her Romeo had known she was there-- "But soft! What light through yonder window breaks? It is the East and Juliet is the Sun!" Barbara felt she might as well feed that poor stray-- she was awake anyway. When the deed was done she returned inside to find Bernie good as gold and proud as a tin toy soldier.

Barbara wondered if there could possibly be a connection between Bernie's maladjusted attitude and Gray cat's hunger. Until the stray's needs were met, Bernie not only acted naughty but would also refuse to consume his supper. No more hysterical pacing or menacing mimicry just as long as his female guest had been fed... how simple could it be? So the solution to the greatest mystery of the 20th century had been solved. Bernie, the gallant gentleman that he was, could not attain inner harmony or tranquility until his paramour was nourished and nurtured.

The previously peaceful home was now back to normal. Bernie always knew when Gray cat was outside and Barbara would do her part by keeping the food bowl full. In the daytime their tete a tete was he on the balcony and she below in the garden. Evenings found him pressed against the windowpane gazing at her silhouetted shadow in the moonlight.

He would tirelessly scan the horizon for Gray cat, every fiber of his being and sensory perception acutely taut and fine-tuned to catch the hint of her scent, the rustle of her fur, the slightest murmur from her throat. No sentry posted on guard duty could have been more dedicated or diligent. In all this time, their noses never once touched as there was always a door or screen to separate them, but the lack of physical contact didn't seem to bother them. They conveyed their affection through adoring eyes and this bond connected two sensitive souls.

Confidence began to grow in the disillusioned stray

as she eventually allowed herself to be touched and even groomed. The horribly sticky mess that had cocooned her fur and restricted normal movement had to be cut off, as it was a substance repellant to soap and water. It was accomplished by a manicured trim done each day while she was preoccupied with her socializing. Gray cat's body weight began to stabilize and trust was evident in the simple act of her laying in the sunshine by their back door.

Eventually Barbara was allowed the privilege of picking her up and it was discovered that she was a HE and Gray cat (alias Juliet) was actually a Jules. Oh well, so much for the romantic Shakespearean comparison. Jules or Juliet, it didn't make any difference to Bernie; he had a friend and that is what mattered to him.

Spring melted into summer and Gray cat became a steady boarder at Barbara & Bernie's Bed and Breakfast. He never ventured inside the house but was always close by and became her 'yard cat' observing her while she gardened and cared for her lawn. He found perfect peace there and considered it his home, but when he wandered beyond her property, trouble and danger lurked nearby.

The saddest thing about unwanted strays is the abuse they must endure from the cat haters. These people seem to think they are entitled to inflict vicious cruelty on starving cats under the premise of protecting birds. How can they feel kindness in abundance to one species while they torture and punish the other? Surely they must see the contradiction in their actions. They are all God's creatures, in need of compassion and placed on earth for our enjoyment and pleasure. This gift is so purely innocent, that any abuse of it is surely a sin.

The neighborhood stories began to circulate about Gray cat. Rocks where thrown to keep him off a lawn and poison was hinted as a final deterrent. Then there was the morning he showed up with a bloody wound on the brow of his face. Barbara called desperately voicing her despair. "What are we going to do with Gray cat? How can we keep him safe from those self righteous neighborhood thugs?"

She had asked her vet if possibly Bernie needed a 'friend' and sadly he told her no, Bernie didn't need another cat, he was perfectly happy alone. If she wanted another pet, go ahead and take in the stray. So, that little piece of information seemed to close the door forever on Gray cat from becoming a permanent part of her household and Barbara from ever knowing the joy of watching the daily interaction of multiple cats.

Summer slipped by and the cool autumn breezes whipped through Gray cat's now daily combed fur. He was physically fit and well fed, but beginning to feel lonely as his human friend had been driven inside by the onset of cool temperatures. He had begun to wander over to our house and would sit on the rail outside our windows observing our cats who where intently looking out at him.

We so wanted Barbara to adopt this child of the streets but understood her situation. Gray cat and Bernie seemed to be great friends from afar, but might be mortal enemies once enclosed within the same four walls-- and living with two intolerant cats could be more than mild mannered Barbara could bear.

We were all trying to find a home for him but the weather situation was getting too frosty for our tolerance. One cold night we broke down and brought him in. We placed him in a downstairs bathroom where he snuggled deep into a bed of blankets and between cold and nervous shivers fell sound asleep. Still uncertain what we were going to do with him, we let him have the run of our lower level with no interference from the dogs or cats. He quickly found the couch and seemed to be completely at home. We named him 'Harm' in honor of a wonderful cousin of ours who had recently passed away. Our cousin had always joked that when he died he was going to come back as some little pampered poodle or cat and sit on peoples' laps while soaking in all that wonderful petting and stroking. Well, it so happened that the very first time Gray cat let me pick him up was the same day that our cousin Harm passed away. Always shy of me before, when I held him he was as calm and relaxed as any of our cats that have been handled for years.

I held my breath in anticipation of Gray cat's future. My poor animal saturated husband most certainly did not want another cat. Somehow the thought of six cats underfoot—prowling and stalking made him kind of queasy. Still, how could he turn the namesake of a favorite cousin out into the winter elements? Couldn't be done! So off to the vet for a little visit and home again neutered and never to be cold again. How lovely for Gray cat and also cousin Harm.

Welcome Harm cat. Let me introduce you to Drake, Riley, Pumpkin, Katie, Wheeler, Bubba, Rowdy, Dexter, Bambi, Dukie, Dusty and Pedro. We have made you our baker's dozen-- number 'thirteenth' signature on the Christmas cards. Here are some words of wisdom given to you from the other five cats:

1. You will never go hungry, as the food bowls are always full. But the parrot is definitely off limits; he is not a part of the food chain.

2. Dad always saves some milk for us from his breakfast cereal every morning. First come first served, but tap him on the leg if he forgets.

3. You can sleep anywhere in the house and are allowed on all the furniture but snoring cats are escorted out of the bedroom at night.

4. Pumpkin is STILL called 'the baby,' even though he is way bigger than most of us, and no matter what he does, he *never* gets in trouble.

5. Don't even think of eating out of Bubba's food bowl. He hasn't learned 'sharing' yet and likely has no intention to do so.

So Harm, we are overjoyed to have you join our clan and by all means, please feel free to place your paw prints upon our hearts.

BEN AND POOCH

THE SADDEST STORY EVER TOLD

This is the story about a young boy, his dog, and the circumstances by which they were parted. It is one of the saddest tales that I have ever heard and cannot be told without a flood of pent up emotions surfacing and ravaging the psychological balance of the storyteller. After almost fifty years, the feelings are still so raw that when exposed, it results in an uncontrolled breakdown of tears and soul encompassing agony.

The boy in the story is my husband, Ben, and the dog that it centers around was named Pooch. My husband is clearly a hypersensitive person when it comes to the well being of animals, especially strays or those in dire need. He is a champion for the underdog... literally. There is no animal he will not rescue and cannot bypass even a caterpillar crawling midway on a busy bike trail without stopping and escorting it out of danger's way. When we encounter an animal in trouble he is always the first to suggest we take it home with no hesitation for the inconvenience we might be courting. I, on the other hand, am always weighing the added work factor but not Ben. He seems led down this path with an overwhelming devotion to accommodate their needs.

Ben's father was a hardworking, industrious businessman employed as a manager for a large chain store. His dedication was evident in the long hours and attention to every detail of the retail business. He loved this job and took extreme pride in his many accomplishments and successes. Being a merchant meant early hours and late nights but it was to ensure a brighter future for his family and so the career became his top priority.

Ben's mother was a happy homemaker involved in every part of her children's lives. She was a supportive spouse, socially active in community, church, civic affairs and quite content with her role. Ben had a younger sister five years his junior and the difference in their ages created a huge gap in the things they had in common. This typical eleven-year-old boy lived for Cowboys and Indians, riding his bike, exploring for turtles and lizards in the creek, and playing ball.

It was a good solid middle class life that they were living as they enjoyed the prosperity of the times that were available to this conventional American family. But in spite of all this, Ben was a lonely boy. His father was gone before he arose in the morning and usually came home long after he was in bed asleep, but Ben did not pine for fatherly affection. They spent Sundays together and planned that day around family activities that started with a large breakfast before church, dinner at a local restaurant, and always ending the day with a leisurely afternoon drive. They shared the funny papers and occasionally played rough and tumble games. This was enough male attention for Ben at this stage of his life.

His mother was quite attentive to his personal and social needs, planning elaborate birthday parties, and allowing him the freedom a boy this age needed for investigating all the wonders around him. He was given permission to ride off on his bike in the morning with no concern for his whereabouts during the day in an era when parents gave no thought to predatory dangers.

His father firmly believed in having a family pet and routinely cited that a dog was the best psychologist a family could have, for with a canine as a counselor they would never need a second opinion. So, man's best friend was always a part of their family portrait and whereas they all felt affection for it, Ben routinely gave his entire heart and soul over to his domesticated confidant. A pup was never just a pet to him but much, much more.

It was very common to see dogs running loose in those days before leash laws and their strict enforcement. Many people would simply release a litter of pups or an unwanted dog by the side of a highway trusting someone would come along and rescue them. Such was the fate of a male hound dog puppy, which was wandering along an auxiliary highway in the countryside outside of East St. Louis, Illinois. Ben's family out for a Sunday drive could not resist the temptation of the desperately frightened highway vagabond and stopped to pick up the helpless hitchhiker.

Each individual was fond of the newest passenger but the pre-teen boy in the back seat had just met the joy of his life. The puppy instinctively knew that of the four members in the car that afternoon, the young boy was to be his and his alone. From that day forward no one else mattered to either one of them. They needed only each other. They were brothers. Human and canine most definitely, but brothers just the same. This boy and dog could have provided a subject for a Norman Rockwell classic painting. Footloose and fancy free, the two were always together as Pooch had become Ben's shadow, not more than just a step away, and his co-pilot on the great adventure of life. They knew each other's thoughts and felt each other's emotions. Never had there been two more closely matched life forms.

A man at the top of his profession can sometimes feel over confident about the good breaks that life was dealing him. Always whispering in his ear was the translucent temptation to just strike out on his own and break away from the constricting rules or petty regulations dictated by the chain store's tyrannical superintendent. That explorer spirit found in all men coupled with the lure of being your own boss could be as intoxicating and alluring as the strongest narcotic. Perhaps it was that one unnecessary directive or a chastising letter from the home office, but the fact was Ben's dad was financially secure and seemed to have the golden touch to become an entrepreneur. All these factors made the decision easier to break away from the restrictions of working for someone else. Why not seek the freedom to explore your own personal vision?

So, the lucrative lifeline was severed and the steady paycheck was foregone as the path strewn with risk-taking chances had been chosen. This savvy businessman's intuition had always been correct before and years of experience, coupled with a great work ethic and the precise knowledge of how to run a profitable business seemed all that was necessary to succeed. It was a time in history when the brave men who took gambles were rewarded with imposing prosperity and mass fortunes were there just for the making.

The newly independent businessman had chosen an excellent location in the center of the heavily trafficked 39th street business district as his field of dreams. The store was stocked with the finest dime-store variety and dry goods available and the new proprietor was brimming with pride and enthusiasm at his first solo endeavor. Everything appeared so promising, the experience so exhilarating, the future so rosy. The business was successful and for two years the seas were calm and peaceful. Then the Devil himself must have dealt the cards for the next hand.

A popular and powerful chain purchased the vacant

storefront right next-door and set about with a vengeance to break the back and crush the very life from this newfound small business owner. They stocked the exact same goods but set their prices so ridiculously low that no profit could have possibly been gleaned from their sales. But profit was not their motive-- they were there to bulldoze the competition, crush their opponent and grind the marrow from the bones of the carcass they were savaging.

Just a game to this giant company and their scoreboard tallied only the cold calculation of dollars, sales, and customer count. It was the age-old power struggle of the strong over the weak, the overseer and the slave, the land baron and the peasant. The end goal was to monopolize all of the business, to dominate the trade and then with all competition gone, set prices as they willed. Their battle cry was "we will not be undersold". To Ben's father, it seemed that his new competitor's mission was to seek out and destroy not just the business but also the man who had the audacity to stand against them. The confident entrepreneur who had so bravely taken the chance of a lifetime was being mentally tortured as he watched the demise of everything he had worked a lifetime for.

While at the store he had to keep up the brave front of the successful businessman, but when he entered the confines of his own home the false bravado deflated. What his family saw was a desperate man drowning in defeat and suffocating from overwhelming fear. He was a proud man doubting his own instincts and fumbling for a foothold as all of his financial assets were being poured down the drain.

His progressive new store with all his innovative ideas and filled with beautiful merchandise stood empty and forlorn while the masses flocked next door to the proverbial wolf in sheep's clothing. Unpaid bills began to mount up, collectors began to hound him for payment and the financial foundation that he had so carefully built to shield his family was being ravished through his unsuccessful efforts to keep the business alive.

Few of us will ever know what it must feel like to go broke, to lose everything that had taken a lifetime to accumulate and stand empty handed when the cup once overflowed. What this horrific experience did to this man could never be expressed through mere words. It not only dashed his self-esteem into shattered splinters but also questioned his competence as a breadwinner. A dark depression came over Ben's father and locked the door of the cell in his self-imposed prison. At the store he made a gallant effort to keep up the pretense that the downturn would reverse itself, but at home the situation was a simple black and white ledger book spread on the table surrounded by piles of unpaid bills and a bank account growing smaller by the day.

The marriage had been enhanced by prosperity and hopeful dreams. They had lived the life of elegant dinner parties, huge employee picnics, the finest furniture, new cars and all the surface trappings that made life so comfortable and people more lovable. When the good times were abundant and money flowed, friends were bountiful and respect seemed to follow those with the flashiest possessions. But all that was evaporating in a puff of smoke as the decay of defeat brought about the wilting and withering of their once flamboyant life style.

How different history would have been if this young couple had lived in today's environment. They would have gone to a financial advisor to discuss their monetary disaster and perhaps he could have alleviated the drain on their personal finances. Dialogue and guidance might have prevented spoken accusations and stopped the unnecessary blame on a blameless situation. No person was actually responsible for this failure, as it would have been impossible to predict the 'conglomerate' sabotage.

But there was no one to help this husband and wife of sixteen years with their personal crisis. This scenario was set in the early 1950's, an era before the advent of talk show psychiatry and the general acceptance of family counseling services. Each family unit was its own little society and family secrets were safeguarded under wraps. When problems developed and the ensuing stress exploded into the household, it was carefully contained within their walls and no hint of trouble was ever allowed to leak out. Close friends or relatives were kept at bay and in the dark from any of the details as the difficulties began to fester and decay the root of their marital relationship.

A cancer-like disease known as stress spilled over from their lives into the daily existence of their children through the constant bickering about their dilemma. They tried to shield them from the truth but even the simple act of smiling was no longer a part of their family interactions. It was the way things were done back then... cloak and disguise your feelings while putting on a brave front for the outside world to see. But how could anyone hide the fact that their hearts were being ripped from their bodies while they were sinking in quick sand and all their gallant efforts seemed in vain? Their masks of despair looked like frightening Halloween goblins to the questioning eyes of their children, who had never seen such distorted expressions, heard such hateful accusing tones or felt so alone and frightened. And to further the deception, they were told that things were fine, 'just fine' and not to worry.

Somewhere in all the untruths and turmoil, young Ben began to realize that all was not well and he began to doubt the answers they were giving him. The smoke screen was too obscure for a young boy to see through but he knew better than to ask direct questions. It was wiser to just go along with the charade.

Ben's home life was misery but his school experience was even worse. When they had moved to the new house at 4047 Magnolia Place he had been required to change schools. No longer cocooned by the friendly neighborhood at #2 Sherwood Forest in quiet Belleville, he was stepping into an inner-city snake pit of hostile peers who hated him just because he wasn't from the tough neighborhoods they came from. At a time when he needed encouragement and acceptance he found rejection and scorn.

School was unbearable in itself, but the walk to and from became a daily rigor akin to facing a firing squad. His route to school crossed unfriendly territory and the bullies singled out Ben as their whipping boy and punching bag. He knew not one happy moment in his day for there was no reprieve from his hellish suffering, save for his one and only friend.

Through all this Ben had Pooch, still as solid and strong hearted as ever, never changing and always true blue. A tight hug around his neck prompted a wag from his tail that coated the bruised and scarred feelings, calmed the racing heart and cooled the knot in his aching stomach. As long as Pooch was with him, Ben could bear the burden set upon his shoulders.

Nighttime was the worst for Ben as darkness was his enemy. Sleeplessness had become worse than a nightmare and while lying awake he was bombarded by the hushed, angry and arguing voices of two miserable strangers that once had been his loving parents. It felt as though his bed had become a coffin and he was being buried alive-- screaming for help-- but only his brain could hear him yell. A stomach clutched in pain, a throat constricted by fear, eyes brimming with tears, and a small boy forever marred by these circumstances. The only comfort in this dark abyss was that steadfast, shaggy body snuggling against him with a moist nose and large floppy ears. Poochie was the only one that could temporarily stop the pain and it was the warmth of him lying close by that finally lulled Ben off to sleep.

In this time of strife, Pooch was the sanity in Ben's world. To some he might have been just another longhaired mutt but now he had became the trusted child psychologist, that spiritual advisor, the candle in the dark that Ben so desperately needed for security.

School days for Ben brought social paralysis. He had numbed to all external events to the extent that all he could do was count the hours until the weekend. Those two glorious days were the only joy in Ben's life. That was when he became the Lone Ranger whisking along on his bike named the Green Hornet and Pooch became Tonto his trusty sidekick running faithfully alongside. They were a team… best buddies who seemed to merge into one body as they bravely ventured into the world to fight injustices.

But a new restriction at home had Pooch protesting his own injustice. New leash laws were being enforced to curb the menacing packs of stray dogs that had begun to plague the St. Louis area. Because of the fines that could be levied for having a loose dog, Pooch now was being tied to a tree in the backyard or confined to the basement while Ben was at school. His days of complete freedom were being curtailed and he displayed his displeasure by barking constantly until Ben returned home.

Soon, Pooch became an accomplished escape artist, the Houdini of the dog chain and it became harder and harder to keep him under lock and key when he wanted free. Once loose, he made it a habit of heading over to the neighbor's lawn and depositing his gift to the crabby lady that lived next door. She was always snooping out her window and would catch the perpetrator in the act then bolt outside yelling and waving her arms in exaggerated alarm. Why Pooch always went on her lawn was a mystery but she seemed to lay in wait until it was done so she could make a scene and cause a commotion for everyone in the neighborhood to witness.

It was this theatrical display, the arms frantically pointing and the bellowing alarm that was the straw that broke the overburdened camel's back. Ben's family had no particular loyalty to this busy body neighbor. She was an unlikable sort who could neither tolerate children or animals but what they could not face was one more problem, not even a little one like a renegade dog doing what comes naturally. It was the stress of dealing with a harsh personality that magnified the severity of the indiscretion into mammoth proportions. They just wanted to silence the complaints; the over the fence gossiping, the hyper antics, but mostly they just wanted to stop the pain.

And so they reacted-- retreated actually-- and bowed to the demands of the demented neighbor and resigned themselves to call animal control to take the offender away. It would be the quickest and most permanent solution to quiet the nagging neighbor's relentless assault on them.

The exact conversation when they told Ben about their decision to remedy the problem by eliminating the family pet has been lost to history. I am sure that when he heard the words ' Pooch' and 'Dog Pound' the roar of blood to his ears drowned out any words of explanation or logic that tumbled from his parent's lips and tear-filled eyes obscured their concerned expressions. All his senses had short-circuited save one... intense searing pain. Nothing they could say would ever have made that decision right. Surely, they were not going to give a faithful member of the family away for such an innocent misdeed and especially not at the insistence of such a disagreeable neighbor. But they had made their final decision and all the worn out clichés rolled off their tongues like butter on a hot skillet. "It was for the best." "They would find him a good home in the country where he could run." "He would be happier."

A knife made of words killed their little boy that day and the events that followed twisted it deeper into his soul and psyche than an earthquake ripping open the earth. They were too blinded by their financial problems to see their own fragile child crumbling and withdrawing before their very eyes.

The next morning was a school day when the dogcatcher's truck pulled up in front of the house. Ben had no choice except to say his despondent good-byes to his only real friend... one whom he clearly loved even more than his parents. The man in the uniform, that horrible excuse for humanity must have deeply hated dogs for just the sight of him caused Pooch to recoil in terror. What was there about this man? What aura or scent telegraphed to the canine what was waiting at the end of their caged ride? How could they sense what their doom was to be? Was it death and misery that this man breathed out into the daytime air or was it just so intense a hatred for the helpless that it eked out his pores like a festering abscess?

Brave Poochie, always the friendliest fellow on the block, refused to go with this man. He looked at this figurehead and could not detect any human blood beating through his veins. His face registered only coldness and cruelty. And those eyes... they could actually look at that broken-hearted boy clinging to his shivering companion and show no pity. He could not feel the slightest sympathy for the wounds that this scene was ripping into the future emotions of the innocent and voiceless victims. This public employee felt nothing. He was doing his job and the faster done the better. He had a day full of capturing strays and delivering them to the death house.

"Get in the truck, you filthy cur." The voice was that of a living devil and it chilled the very air around him. Poochie looked into that face without a soul and saw the specter of death, the white horse of the apocalypse, the bottomless pit of Hades. This lovable pooch, never one to disobey an order, for once in his life became defiant. "No, he would not go with this person, he belonged here with his people... with his boy, Ben."

"Lady, tell the kid to get that dog in the truck or I won't take him." So just like mechanical robots, good law-abiding citizens and pillars of society, they complied with the hissed command. Ben ordered his dearest friend to jump into the back of the truck and Poochie, completely trusting his master, faithfully obeyed.

The steel door slammed shut, the vehicle drove away and a confused face looked out the rear window and implored. "Is this what you wanted me to do?'

How the angels must have wept when they witnessed that scene. A child had just betrayed the love of his life. He had become the Judas to a gentle, trusting Jesus and delivered him into the hands of the most heartless of enemies. In Kahlil Gilbran's spiritual writings from his book *The Prophet*, a Woman spoke, saying, "Tell us of pain." And he said, "Your pain is the breaking of the shell that encloses your understanding. Even as the stone of the fruit must break, that its heart may stand in the sun, so must you know pain." Maybe this heart-wrenching episode was necessary in this young mortal's life to shape the person that he was intended to become.

"Now off to school, Ben." The most tragic event to

ever befall him and now he had to buck up and face the world like it hadn't really happened, push the pain down into himself and put on a happy face for all the world to see. Every emotion within him shut down, his very faith in justice had been breached, and the chemistry that directed his life changed that day. Yes, his heart was still pumping blood to his body-- his lungs were supplying oxygen and his brain was still capable of figuring his daily math assignments. But the boy that once needed-- no, more than needed, relied and depended on Pooch to help withstand the rigors of his troubled life was now facing the future without him and it was more than he could bear.

The day progressed, school was finally out and Ben returned home. He felt no need to raise his eyes from his downward gaze; there was no light or hope for him. He was only a kid. He had no voice, no rights, just as powerless as the animals. And then he saw him... standing on the front porch... wagging, smiling and laughing. He had come home. Pooch was back! There was a God in heaven and prayers from little boys could be answered. Ben had promised everything-- bartered with God to never do anything wrong ever again just to have this one wish-- Pooch back in his arms. It was a fairy tale ending to a very bad dream. The encounter between dog and boy was as pure as any miracle imagined. Ben buried his tear-stained face in Poochie's soft fur and embraced the warm body that meant more to him than life itself.

The happy reunion was sadly short lived and bittersweet. Ben soon found out that Pooch had not been given a reprieve to be returned to the good graces of the family but instead had escaped from the prison wagon when the warden opened the door and had made a mad dash toward freedom. He was many miles from Magnolia Place and not familiar with the area but was determined to get back to his people and spent the entire day searching for the scent that would lead him home.

This is the part of the story where you wish there was some divine intervention and a guardian angel would voice a decree that this dog and boy could never be separated again. They truly belonged together. There was a purpose for their union, a reason why these two soul mates had found one another. Surely the saints and deceased ancestors watching over this family were hoping and praying that this miraculous escape would be rewarded with a happy ending and in a 'perfect world' it would be so. But it was not to be. You see--- these earth bound parents had no revelation that a spirit might have opened the door and guided Pooch homeward. The armor around their hearts could not be penetrated as they witnessed the poignant reunion, and if they had been touched by an angel, they never knew it.

The dogcatcher returned the next morning and the only blessing was that Ben and Pooch had one more night together. The dreaded truck arrived and the same evil man was summoned to replay the nightmare that had been staged just the day before. Ben again was ordered to coax the escaped prisoner back into the metal cell and this time both boy and dog knew Pooch would not be coming back. The wicked jailer would not be out-smarted by this clever dog again.

The sound of a dying soul was relayed by a helpless human voice tearfully begging 'please no'. But to those at the scene, it had just become so much background noise. After all, what could possibly express the utter despair of a boy who was dealing with the guilt that he was betraying his beloved dog for the second time? It was a sorrow too intense for someone so young to be asked to experience.

The last scene of this drama has been frozen forever

in Ben's memory. Pooch... eyes locked on him as that truck departed for the final journey. They were never to see one another again and neither would ever understand why this had happened to them. Ben would spend the rest of his life wondering, just wondering what become of his dear, sweet Poochie.

Life trudged on. Ben's father lost the store but would not declare bankruptcy and instead spent his entire lifetime paying back his debts and preserving his pride. His mother went to work to help with the bills and support the family. Her days of leisure had ended as she entered the work force never fully accepting the junction that her life had taken. The family packed up the remaining inventory from their now defunct store and headed hundreds of miles away to start over in a modest family run enterprise in a much smaller community. Through the years, many pets came through the household, but none would ever replace Pooch in Ben's heart.

It was only recently that Ben could finally relate the complete story of Pooch. He had buried those painful facts so deeply inside himself that he simply would not allow them to come to the surface. When he did talk through the entire account, there was the realization that he had never healed from the trauma. The wound was clearly as painful now as it had been then. When telling the story, he becomes that young boy and re-lives all that misery once again.

I have said to Ben, perhaps I should not write Pooch's story and if I did, not share it with friends or for publication. It would be written just for him. But he stated that as painful as it would be to see this hurtful adolescent memory in print, perhaps it would prevent another child from going through a similar hardship. If only one parent could read this narrative and realize that by giving away the family pet they may be removing the only security blanket between that child and utter despair-- it would be his gift to mankind.

Parents, please protect your children from devastating occurrences, guarding them from physical, mental, and emotional destruction. Let them talk freely and honestly value their feelings, for what goes seriously wrong in childhood follows them into adulthood and their disillusions become the ball and chain that forever weighs down their lives.

Now as an adult, Ben can see the entire scenario from a parent's point of view. He can better understand his father's grievous predicament and the stranglehold it had on their family. His parents never neglected the physical needs of their children, but they just did not have the insight to understand the deep-seated emotions within their son.

How lovely it would have been if they had said, "Since Pooch found his way back home, we will just keep him and try harder to control the potty habits. And if by chance, he should soil the neighbor's yard, we will hurry over to pick up his indiscretion and bring a plate of cookies to Mrs. Crabapple as our sincere apology". History would have been forever changed and an innocent boy would never again be haunted by those sad brown eyes embracing him for the last time.

In my heart I truly do believe that one day Ben and Poochie will return in *spirit form* to ride and run not only through the streets of St. Louis but over the hills and valleys yet to be explored. Their battered, anguished feelings will be long forgotten and a lifetime of grieving will once more see happy trails again. Benny and Poochie, together forever.

THE DUKE AND DUCHESS OF EDGEWOOD HILLS

OUR RABBIT HABIT

Bunnies--they are undisputedly God's most perfect creation. Truly the softest, sweetest and most gentle species to have ever hopped across this green earth and right into our hearts. Just a virtual little muff of love packaged into a miniature, compact container the exact size and shape of cradling arms. No entanglement of gangling limbs to deal with, their extremities are all neatly folded beneath them and securely tucked away to conform to their oval shape. None of those skinny, scrawny, bony necks affixed to most life forms that hideously protrude like a periscope tottering unsteadily in the breeze. These elegant truffles of fur display just the slightest pinnacle to support that noble head tightly embraced by their body. A bunny's entire torso is expertly sculptured into the oblong shape of a Faberge egg and the ultimate embellishment on this lively bundle is the perfect pompon of a tail that perkily perches like a downy cloud of cotton candy at the bottom most spot of their gracefully arched back.

The demeanor of a rabbit's joy is never an uncontrollable whip or wag of its tiny tail but dispassionately exhibited by the self-restrained vibrations of a velvety, petite nose. And those eyes-- why, they are an open window to its soul. Large, round and honest they create the earnest expression of such pristine purity that just a glance is capable of melting the steeliest iceberg around even the most cynical heart. No sly, sneaky, feline smirk on this flawless face. Theirs is a look of mild surprise mixed with an air of enchanting glee.

All this precise refinement is enclosed in that irresistibly touchable, bunny fur, as sensuous as the ultra silkiness of a satin pillow. So soft in fact, fingertips are much too course to completely appreciate and only the stroking caress against one's cheek can fully perceive the phenomenon of such an exquisite outer garment. Only their ears betray their finely crafted image, but perhaps they were fashioned with just a hint of humor by the Creator to remind us that absolute perfection is not obtainable on this earthly sphere. Charming, quiet, shy, and demure, most assuredly they are the twinkle of God's eye. And to Him I say 'Thank You,' for he outdid himself when he masterminded that delightful deity called Bunny.

After an introduction like that, one might imagine that I had been born and raised in the middle of a litter of rabbits, but it was not so. A dog, cat and parakeet were my childhood playmates and the thought of owning a real live cottontail never entered my mind. So who, you ask, turned me on to bunnies? It was my "I must own that rabbit," spouse, and this is how the story unfolds.

One Saturday afternoon Ben and I decided to go antiquing. We rambled through the rural countryside scouring it for hidden treasures tucked away in some obscure shop off the main highway and byway. A large red barn, which was the showcase for a faded sign espousing old-fashioned collectibles stored within, seized our attention and a quick, bumpy, U-turn, headed us toward our destiny. We felt like children when given free rein in an amusement park. It was the thrill of the hunt that motivated us—the need to find that unique and rare relic so bathed in historical significance. We yearned to uncover pieces of Americana, belonging to the past, yet reaching out to the present. Old furniture seemed to tell their tales and stories by the faded nicks and battle scars that life had etched upon it along the way.

The establishment was open and we tentatively searched the piles of knickknacks as we caressed the rusty and worn items in a virtual quest for the authenticity of the dusty and threadbare. An ancient washing machine beckoned from beneath a forgotten pile of rubble and after a few minutes of bargaining it was to be ours. We dragged the monstrosity out the door as the proprietor, hoping to detain us a few minutes longer called out after us, "Don't forget to tour the animal barn". Those seven words changed our lives forever.

We ventured into the musty, damp atmosphere of the large farm building as our eyes slowly adjusted to the dim, muted light. Suddenly, right before us were cages and cages of the most picturesque and lovely baby bunnies ever witnessed by humankind. We had been expertly ambushed and had swallowed the bait-- hook, line and sinker. Then came the innocent question, "Would you like to hold one?" The spider should consider taking lessons from this crafty individual the next time it has trouble snaring a fly in its web. Surely there would be no harm in holding just one little soft, needy baby bunny for a few moments. That familiar phrase 'just say no' never entered our minds.

The instant that delectable powder puff was placed in Ben's hands, a knowing smile spread across the farmer's face. Standing before him was the all-time perfect mark, sitting duck, bear-bait, and Mr. Soft Touch. I peered into Ben's glazed eyes and suggested that perhaps we should think about this, but my words evaporated into thin air as he was already inquiring about all the details we needed to raise this fur muffin into our first 'house bunny'.

So these dyed in the wool dog owners became mama and daddy to the most gorgeous bunny we had ever seen. She was a champagne colored, female French Lop with a hint of sable trim, huge, brown puppy-dog eyes and endowed with the longest, plushest, adorably floppy ears ever known to frame such an angelically stunning face. On the drive back we petted and talked to her while wondering what name could possibly describe this regal creature. She had an aura of royalty, so dignified and majestic that the name Duchess seemed fitting.

We brought her home to our canine dominated world and she set about letting us all know that life with Duchess had just begun. While trying to gently introduce her to our two Dobermans, out from underneath the kitchen table she bolted and viciously bit each dog on their hind leg then dashed back into the shadows. The dogs were impressed, really impressed, and from that day forward were frightened to death of her. They tiptoed through the house in nervous anticipation, for they never knew when the stealth bomber bunny might ambush them. Both would become shaking cowards whenever she was near and bolt in a complete panic at the mere wiggle of her nose. Little did we know that inside the rabbit 'Trojan horse' we brought home from the farm were the multiple personalities of Attila the Hun, and the Robo-Bunny Terminator. Our kingdom was soon to be sacked.

But she knew that she had us wrapped around her furry little rabbit foot. Litter box trained and free to roam anywhere in the house, Duchess loved to hop up on the couch and watch TV with us in the evenings. She would hunker down in our laps for her full body massage while making little squeaking noises to show her pleasure. Heaven forbid if we should stop caressing her. Her annoyance was displayed by a bite to our stomach as her command to get us to resume. Ben now had a waistline filled with new bellybuttons and held as much respect for her temperament as did the dogs.

Duchess was the only bunny of the seven house rabbits we eventually owned that had this biting habit. Most bunnies would not think of using aggression for they are peaceful and gentle souls. Duchess just happened to feel that she was the boss and enforcing the rules meant corporal punishment to her.

In the mornings, Duchess would hear our alarm go off and come racing down the hallway full speed ahead— filled with joy-- eager to greet us and the new day. I would call out "Bunny on the run" to warn the dogs and announce her welcome arrival.

How we loved that rabbit! We nicknamed her our little honey bunny and melted in adoration every time we saw her. She chewed holes in all of our clothes, severed phone lines, bit lamp cords in half and gnawed on our antique wooden furniture at every opportunity. As we were discovering all this destruction, we could not imagine it could come from such an innocent looking angel. Putting up barricades seemed like a good solution but this one could jump. Worse yet, a stubborn determination fueled by a will of iron propelled this tenacious bunny. When God was giving out the 'gentle and docile' characteristics, she was busy conquering the carrot patch and besides, she liked being feisty, brash and more feared than a pit bull.

As much as we adored Duchess, one dose of her was plenty. Neither of us entertained the thought of buying her a companion and she seemed perfectly content with her position as dominatrix of the empire.

Some months later, on a pristine spring morning with just a nip of winter still in the air, we decided to take an early morning ride out to Rock Cut State Park, a recreational area about six miles from our house. Strolling down to the shoreline of the water we lustily drank in the vision of the mist rising off the lake's surface. Both of us stood breathlessly spellbound as we eavesdropped on the lifestyles of the occupants living about the water's edge. Turtles stretched out on fallen oaks appeared as if they were working on their tans in the hazy sunbeams while monstrous bullfrogs balanced precariously on paper thin lily pads. A battalion of ducks paddled furiously toward us in hopes of an early morning nibble and dragonflies helicoptering overhead heralded their importance to the ecological balance.

We motionlessly stalled there, desperately trying to blend in to the landscape, but our deception fooled none of the marshland neighborhood occupants. We loomed hugely awkward and held no hopes of competing with their perfect environmental camouflage. After getting our fill of watching the water aerobics, we contently hiked up the hillside to our awaiting van and the half-hour ride home.

Strapped in and headed outward from the parking lot we traveled about ninety feet when Ben abruptly applied the brakes. We both just sat transfixed at what we were simultaneously witnessing. Sitting centered in the middle of that tar-black roadway was a huge, radiantly white, bundle of breathlessly, beautiful bunny. This was no wild, brown, wiry, untamed rabbit but a storybook character, a pet store prodigy domestically bred for refinement. It was as clean and well groomed as any photogenic rabbit posed on a calendar layout or the eye-catching centerpiece of a seasonal Easter greeting card.

We were transfixed in time and stared in complete disbelief at this utter breach of nature. Outdoor enthusiasts that we were, it was incomprehensible to us how this snowy-white bunny could possibly be sitting on this exact spot at this precise moment in our lives. Just five minutes earlier or later and our paths would never have crossed. If it had been a deer or raccoon we would have been thrilled to glimpse them in their natural habitat, but this rotund, pristine show bunny made both of us take a reality check at what we had just stumbled across. We were in Alice's wonderland and the fairy tale rabbit had made its presence known. He looked surreal-- like a child's stuffed toy that had somehow been accidentally dropped.

This little one was completely out of its comfort zone as he sat there on the tarmac, ears upright and alert. He did not display the body language of the typical woodland animal surprised by a human presence. The expression on his face was one of forlorn abandonment, confusion and disorientation. He didn't bolt to the side of the highway and duck into the concealing greenery, but chose instead to brave the blacktop exhibition in a desperate attempt to seek help. Hiding would have been the instinctual thing to do, but this spunky trooper had mustered up all his courage to sit fully exposed to any and all dangers in his frantic call for assistance.

We surmised he had not been out in the wild very long for he didn't appear to be cold or tattered with debris, but perhaps just one night was enough to tell him this was not the playground he belonged on. This hutch dweller had known only the comforting security of a metal cage and the confusion of open spaces, huge towering trees, and mossy undergrowth did not feel like freedom to him, but more like being trapped in the tangled maze of a haunted forest. Surrounded by celery-colored green foliage contrasted with the dark, woody brown of soggy tree limbs, all traces of snow had long melted and the only object of white in this entire forest preserve was poised several feet in front of us.

Before assuming the role of rescuers, Ben and I both came to the identical conclusion. 'Dumped'-- and this little dumpee was in really serious trouble. Rabbits raised in captivity are not as streetwise as the average cat or dog that is cast aside. A bunny's survival instincts don't offer the same skills as most of nature's wild critters and it knows only to look for the proverbial food bowl filled with alfalfa pellets. It eventually would starve to death even if it were sitting in a field of clover. Nearly every animal is an enemy to the rabbit and whereas most species will fight to defend their lives, the bunny's only defense is to flee in complete terror. Although equipped with powerful, sharp teeth, most never take an offensive stand, but once caught, helplessly submit to their demise. A nervous system so delicate, they can literally die from being startled by an unexpected loud noise and a heart so gentle, it simply gives up the will to live.

So, operation Bunnygate sprang into action. Creeping out of the van doors in exaggerated slow motion, we silently sneaked closer and closer to our conquest. Words were spoken softly and reassuringly to quell the fear in the immobilized youngster who was watching our comedic antics. The dance of pursuit had begun. Tiptoe, tiptoe, stop while he would respond with hippity, hoppity, hop. First to the right and then to the left, it was the intricate line dance that could result in the life or death of one frightened, forsaken bunny. There were no abrupt or rapid movements from either party, and his lack of action convinced us that he wanted to be rescued but wasn't quite brave enough to submit. This timid, white bunny with the huge imploring eyes was pleading for our help, but the time spent in the forest preserve had spun him into a bewildered state. He knew humans, just not these humans and we could see he was trying to determine if we could be trusted with the safekeeping of his life.

The game of keep away had already lasted a full twenty minutes as we were becoming increasingly concerned that perhaps our efforts would fail and he would choose the traumatizing woods over us. We had nearly lost hope when strategist Ben came up with a brilliant plan. His childhood obsession with watching cowboy movies was at long last going to be put to the ultimate test. Using the old cattle rustler's ploy of circling around behind the intended prey, we sandwiched him between us. Unfortunately, this crafty outlaw bunny must have seen the same motion pictures, as he was not going to be out-smarted by these bungling tenderfoots. We needed a new plan since this rabbit was too clever for the cowboys, so Ben decided we would become the Indians and trick this nimble-footed desperado the native-American way. He skillfully blended into the foliage and became one with the tree-filled undergrowth. Then, backtracking into the deep woods he silently sneaked up on the fugitive who was intent on watching me. With a swoop of his Eagle-like talons and a warrior's yell, Injun Ben was victorious.

In his hands he held a grateful, indebted soul and as he placed him in my lap there was not the slightest struggle from our newest orphan, but just a sigh of relief and heartfelt gratitude. Human arms had hugged this bunny before, as he wiggled himself into an upright position and snuggled deep into my neck. Clearly, whoever had owned him had spent many hours tenderly cuddling him. His questioning eyes and quivering nose searched for clues about these new people but he must have decided we looked and smelled agreeable because he showed no fear or apprehension as we headed homeward.

The first order of business was selecting the appropriate name for our bashful foundling. We were bringing him home to our lovely Duchess and surely he was as regal as she, so we knighted him 'Sir Duke' as he became the second half of our debonair couple. But the name Duke was just a bit too formal for this precocious and brave hearted male so 'Dukie' became his nickname and he liked it immediately.

At home the dogs sniffed the newcomer, but they personally did not care that much for rabbits as they knew behind that dewy-eyed facade housed a vicious set of sharp incisors. They could take him or leave him, but if he was anything like Duchess they preferred to keep their distance. We placed Dukie in a spare cage with food and water as likely no morsel of substance had passed his lips since his adventure had begun. He was extremely tired and not even curiosity could keep his eyes from succumbing to slumber.

His first sight when he did awaken was the stunning vision of a very confident female rabbit sizing him up from outside his enclosure. Noses touched, whiskers sensed, and two compatible bunny strangers became fast friends. What joy and jubilation for the previously lonely hearts that now were a couple. They inhaled the delicious odors of each other with an eye toward courtship, but were kept separated until Dukie was neutered. Once they were allowed to move in together, Dukie was a natural nester as he straightened the bedding to create the perfect padding for his Duchess. She accepted it with great dignity and their roles were permanently established. She was the dragon slayer, always fearlessly guarding the palace and he was the househusband, busy with their domicile comforts and domestic chores.

The story of Dukie cannot end here. There must have been a reason our paths crossed that fateful day and a lesson to be learned from it. Very likely Duke was an Easter gift purchased from a pet store. Perhaps he was a present bought on a whim or impulse of the moment. No retail clerk is instructed to stress the work and commitment necessary to raise any pet, but tiny, baby puppies, kittens, and bunnies continue to grow and their maintenance chores increase in proportion. There is no doubt that Dukie was well cared for and adored by some young child. I imagine him being held in the arms of an adolescent girl and her gentleness shaping his pleasing, trusting personality.

Yet some tremendous tension must have disrupted their lives and as a result little Dukie was considered a burden too great to bear. It could have been a punishment for not keeping the cage clean enough or perhaps the responsibility of caring for a bunny had become work instead of play. Whatever the cause, it was the truly innocent that received the punitive measure. Dukie was not given the option of relocating with another family but released into a habitat more cold-hearted than captivity. These parents, the role models for their child, took the time and effort to transport him to the sheltered area of the lake and parking lot where they deserted him. While driving away, could they actually have believed that this little bunny that only knew a life in the warm embraces of their child's arms was now ecstatic to be at the mercy of the beasts and burdens of nature?

It is a well-known fact that this scenario happens every day all over the world and it is difficult not to hold ill feelings toward the adults that commit such deeds. Even though realizing that desperate people do desperate things, it is the disillusioned children that often pay as great a price as the forsaken animal. It is their broken hearts longing to be soothed with the knowledge that their animal friend is now secure in a safe environment.

I often envisioned an article in the local paper featuring a large colored picture of Dukie, describing the location where we found him. Just perhaps the now grown little girl would see it and recognize the cherished companion that had known her love for so many months. Maybe then the guilt that clutched her heart and made her feel responsible for his uncertain future would be permanently erased. If that young girl could ever be found, how we would love to place Dukie once more into her aching arms while watching the rejoicing and mending of two broken hearts.

But, out of someone else's tragedy, entered into our lives the most tenderhearted, caring and accepting animal that we have ever known. He sleeps side by side with any cat that needs a warm partner on a cold day, will gladly sacrifice his favorite cracker to another bunny who feels especially hungry, and his entire reason for living seems to be that of giving joyful comfort to humans and animals alike. Dukie... Duchess loves you, and we do too.

THE SPIRIT CAT

SOME THINGS IN THIS WORLD YOU JUST CAN'T EXPLAIN

It was the season of my soul as the journey of my spiritual quest had begun. A personal sojourn to delve deep into the innermost core and scrutinize the fabric of true self. This pilgrimage was to find the origin, the fountainhead, and the wellspring of my inward light. It was a time of peacefulness here at home sedated by the soothing calm of serenity. Our two older dogs, Rowdy and Dexter had finally settled into middle age and that lovely tranquil state where snoozing was the highlight of their day. Puppy Bubba was beginning to control the huge amount of water that hydrated his playful antics and the cats had never been more complacently affectionate. October leaf raking was now just a dusty figment of our imagination and two tired, aching backs had finally begun to straighten into a more human, upright stance.

Marooned inside our toasty nest, the icy fingers of winter were drawing out any warmth that was left in Mother Earth. This timely junction of changing seasons was our chance to play catch-up on the patiently awaiting reading material that beckoned us from its place of repose on bedside tables. Nightfall came early and the silence of the house was filled with creative imaginings that we gleaned from our well worn yet much loved books. It was an opportunity for contemplating inner thoughts and reflecting on the rationalization for our existence. Publications relating to topics such as guardian angels, life after death, and inspirational writings guided us in the search for the goodness in our souls. It was the perfect atmosphere for developing metaphysical communication skills and forging a pathway into a more enlightened sphere. Little did we suspect the stage was being set and the actors cast for the next drama that was to be performed for our benefit.

We had reached yet another milestone in our lives, stepped over our self imposed quota, and had undergone a giant leap into uncertainty by accepting a sixth stray cat into our already abundant feline colony. SIX CATS. It was absurd, irrational, overwhelming, and incorrigible behavior. What would our friends and neighbors think? Worse yet, how do we break the news to our dubious children? We were out of control, teetering on the edge of lunacy and definitely running amok. Perhaps there was a professional support group for people like us, something like ALA, Animal Lovers Anonymous or maybe we were just a phone call away from a public catharsis and the healing wisdom of Oprah. But all this psychobabble we tortured ourselves with did not really matter because the cold hard fact was that number six cat, Harm, had a home and he no longer had to go begging for love.

Positively this was our absolute limit-- both Ben and I agreed. True, we had gone over the top but we could get a handle on this. A solemn vow was taken to subdue ourselves to behave more like the majority of humanity and let the tattered strays move on without so much as an inkling of concern. In an effort to emphasize this firm commitment to our new stance, I felt like ritualizing our decision. There was an urge to march to the communal feeding spot in our front yard, raise both arms while looking skyward and proclaim my determination in a strong and firm voice. "NO MORE!" Whoever or whatever was responsible for directing all the homeless, desperate, needy animals must now stop and desist. The soup line was closed. Lady liberty's light was darkened, and the red carpet had been rolled up and removed. We had done our duty for the animal kingdom, so send them on to the next softhearted family and purge the guilt from our hearts.

I felt confident, strong-willed, and positively unreachable. Nothing was going to melt this stainless steel heart ever again. Besides, we were having a titanic power struggle inside our own four walls. Our lovely, longhaired Harm did not like cats, dogs, birds, or anything that resembled a black garbage bag. What he did love was warm beds, tuna fish, full supper bowls, Italian food and being held on my lap all day.

I tried so hard to gently introduce him to the household routine. One cat at a time with playful activities was the plan. Never before had there been any trouble blending the newest arrival, but this time it was different. Perhaps it was because all the other cats were short haired and sleek while Harm looked like a shaggy, hulking, over-sized grizzly bear. Whatever the cause, they detested him and a monstrous situation grew worse daily.

Our congregation of cats had merged into a single sinister intelligence and that pack mentality was set on taunting the new kid on the block. Harmless Harm would be peacefully looking out the patio door and as I would observe from a pentagon of different directions, five stalking cats, all slowing creeping, bodies held long and low, eyes narrowed, ears flattened, nostrils flared, tails slowly swishing to and fro. It was a horrible sight to witness. Those were my little lovies behaving as hatefully as any legendary villain. Batting, swatting, growling, spitting, biting, pouncing and those were the actions that they would allow me to see. Bullies, all of them, even my lone female Katie, who was usually the fraidy cat, now sashayed and strutted as the gangster's moll of the bad boy's gang. This cat pack showed no mercy and our once nirvana-like household was beseeched by unearthly screams day and night. Certainly not the atmosphere for abstract meditation when the tranquility was pierced by panic strained vocal chords, flying fur and a parade of frenzied cats whizzing by. I was determined to end this territorial skirmish. On went the Mozart music while baby talk flowed like Southern honey and the nihilist instigators were put into isolation, but to no avail. They were all equally guilty as they sneered at my efforts to control them. This militant militia of feline mutants wanted no part of law and order--they loved havoc, discord and mayhem.

Husband Ben jokingly quipped, "No good deed goes unpunished," and suggested maybe we had taken on a challenge that could not be resolved. But then we would get a special little teddy-bear hug from Harm followed by that adoring look that he does so well and our mutual consensus was that we had done the right thing.

Month after month, nothing improved. This band of menacing pointy-eared thugs blocked all litter boxes, food bowls and virtually held hovering Harm prisoner under the old stereo player. Their mental telepathy-like communication controlled the changing of the guard and it was eerie to watch, as one cat would relieve the other of duty. We marveled at their silent understanding of their fiendish plot. I scolded them, shamed them and even used the "NO" word but those five diabolical brains had only one mentality functioning among them and they were absolutely compulsive about it.

As a result, Harm was carried to the eating spot in the kitchen and when he had finished brought to the potty.

Upon closing the door to give him a moment of privacy, I watched as a pride of young lions lined up outside while resting on their haunches waiting for their prey. Often times I would set my armful of Harm in front of the window and if I would step out of the area for even one minute the cat shadows would seep from every corner of the room like an oil slick engulfing the ocean. These Gestapo-like hoodlums were on duty twenty-four hours a day and their solidarity to their evil task was ghoulish.

Then came the night we let Harm stay out in the living room. I found him in the morning cowering from embarrassment and shame. His back end was covered in excrement and his predators had kept him constrained in the center of his odorous accident all night. Those five nighttime marauders had scared more than the daylights out of him and Harm's fear was reaching paranoia dimensions.

We thought we were rescuing him from the perils of nature and now it seemed like Harm was in more jeopardy inside our domain. The only time that he had any real peace was at bedtime when I would bring him into our room and place him on an over-stuffed chair lined with our clothes. He would stay there until the lights were out and then silently sneak to the litter box or the feeding dish. Then when he felt completely safe he would hop up on our California king-sized bed and find a cozy spot between the dogs and us. Sometimes I would wake up in the middle of the night to find Harm sharing my pillow with his paw placed upon my forehead.

My somewhat para-philosopher husband Ben thought I was handling the situation rather poorly. "You are smothering Harm, making him a mama's boy... an emotional cripple. He needs to be a man, find his own way in the household," was his analytical response. So we decided to do it Ben's way and one night after teeth had been brushed and vitamins taken, we brought baby Pumpkin into the bedroom to bond with Harm during the night. It was to be a 'boy's night out' and according to the masculine point of logic, by morning they would be best buddies.

At first, all went well. There was not the tiniest hiss or fuss and I thought Ben was truly a genius, an expert animal psychologist. Then in the early morning dark-- a sound so earth shattering-- we wondered if it was the tornado-warning siren that blasted the quiet of our sleeping den. Arms, legs, dog noses, the entire bed full of body parts leaped upward in unison. Surely it wasn't Gabriel's trumpet sounding the advent of the Armageddon—and hopefully it wasn't the Day of Judgment.

No, nothing as mundane as that. The flick of the light brought us face to face with the noise catastrophe. Harm and Pumpkin were not experiencing inner harmony. They didn't even want to share the same air and instead of finding opposite chairs to meditate on, they had both chosen the same one. The repugnant squall that had shattered our eardrums was their way of letting us know they needed some sensitivity counseling from their Daddy, pet Ph.D.

"GET OUT"!!! Such a command of the English language our resident doctor had. Three A.M. was evidently not the opportune hour for détente as this peace negotiation had just been commandeered by a benevolent dictator, who ceremoniously escorted Pumpkin out of the war zone. A bleary-eyed Ben was not feeling quite so smug about his animal behavior diagnosis and conceded an important lesson that night...sometimes mother knows best. So, with his blessing, Mommy Dearest went back to transporting Harm via the 'arm's express' and we just accepted our weird predicament with resignation.

Nothing could be done to remedy the situation. Harm had no desire or curiosity to even explore and certainly we could understand his hesitation. It was as though he were trekking through a booby-trapped mine field, one misstep and he would be face to face with any one of five, fluffed up, agitated warriors who would pin him to the floor in a pseudo death struggle. We saw enough of this nastiness on the evening news, and surely did not need to have it re-enacted hourly in every corner and crevice of our abode.

Through all our emotional thunderstorms we had privy to one rainbow of enjoyment. In the evenings during our television viewing time when the menagerie of whiskers, tails, and furballs were all finally asleep, we could kick off our shoes and relax. Our reverie of joy was observing the outside activities of the clandestine and covert nocturnal wild creatures that arrived for their nightly tasty tidbits of nourishment. Their presence alone soothed our ruffled feathers and lowered our raging blood pressure. With the front porch light diluting the blackness, we could clearly see those uniquely masked-faces feeding themselves with their human-like tiny hands.

Then on one especially macabre and darkly sinister eve, we spotted an abnormally peculiar looking figure amid the wild ones. It had a soft whitish glow and seemed to appear and disappear in the dark shadows --not unlike what one would expect from a ghostly apparition. Definitely not of this world but per chance a spiritual familiar? Nightly we scoured the inky-black terrain, but as soon as the evasive life-form would appear, it seemed to sense our curiosity-filled, probing eyes and would then dissolve into a fine mist and be gone. We had an overwhelming need to see this phantom of the woodland, but no solid evidence could be provided to ascertain its presence. He was for the time being at least, as uncertified as Big Foot or the Loch Ness sea monster.

So, we hunkered down and prepared ourselves. Armed with binoculars and camouflaged in black sweats, we turned the house lights off. Delectable turkey scraps had been placed in the communal food bowl as a lure for the hungry one. We would see this mysterious creature, or suffer from sleep deprivation trying. It was a challenge that could not be resisted as we lingered anxiously at our posts determined to solve this unsolved mystery.

Then, after hours of waiting, the ghostly shadow appeared. It was no more than an outline on the edge of a misty cloud with its yellow eyes glowing in the diffused light. Our faces were pressed against the window, senses straining to decipher what kind of vapor housed those glassy, piercing orbs. We deduced it was not an albino raccoon, an elusive opossum or a phantasm of the infernal region that emerged from its nether world home to feed on earthly morsels. We could never see quite enough of it to complete the puzzle. Did it walk on two or four legs? Why did all animals scatter abruptly when it appeared? Was it intellectually superior to the other night feeders and perhaps us? Was it dangerous? Questions were all that we had. There were no answers.

As time progressed our expectations grew and imaginations took on a life of their own. It most assuredly had to be some spectacular being skilled in escape and evasion to outsmart us night after night. We knew we had stumbled onto something big... really big and jokingly wondered if we should keep the telephone number of the National Enquirer next to the phone. After all, this could have been the scoop of the century, perhaps the first authentic alien contact or proof positive of the spiritual realm.

Then came "The Night." We had watched for

hours, the stress and anticipation building to a frenzied level when miraculously all elements fell into place. For just one moment the moonlight silently broke through a single clearing in the leaves to spotlight the scene below. There before us, glowing not only from its own inner light but bathed in the illumination of moon glow was the secretive spy, our evasive surprise package, the final solution, the missing link and the reason we had given up the luxury of normal sleep. It was... it was... a CAT!? Another hungry, desperate, four legs with a mouth. Not one word passed between Ben and myself. Did we not remember that vow, our solemn oath? We simply turned on the lights, sat down in our chairs and buried our faces in books.

A cat, of all things. God might have been playing a really good practical joke on us but it was not very funny. I secretly began to call our night wanderer, 'Spirit Cat' but no way was he crossing the threshold to our door. If Pharaoh could harden his heart to the Hebrew slaves, I could do the same when it came to this nomad. And besides I was running out of gas transporting heavy Harm whatever direction he pointed his paw to go. No vacancy-- better yet 'Quarantined' might as well have been posted on the door. No one in -- no one out. We were an island and the boats had all been cut loose from the moorings.

Spirit Cat started coming every evening and even though we acknowledged his presence and worried when he was late, we both knew that enough was enough. Maybe he was just a neighborhood cat that liked to roam, but deep down inside we suspected that was not so. He was there every night, even during those cruel sub-zero spells that were too cold for even the raccoons to brave. As he fed, he would constantly raise his paws to alleviate the frostbite-like pain that brutalized his tender toes as he stood in the deep, bitter snow. So slight of build and delicate of bone, it would take a monster to turn this little one out into these harsh elements. No, there was no one who called him 'baby' and tucked him into a soft *blankie* bed every night.

We had only seen Spirit Cat in the evening hours and never could quite distinguish his luminary characteristics. He was just a vapor in life form that floated in on tiny cat paws and then just shimmered back into the falling, silvery snowflakes. Not orange or white, but more of a golden Harlow blonde color with highlights that glistened and flickered with each fluid motion. Neither tabby striped nor solid but patterned in herringbone tweed, a zigzagging effect that dazzled one's eyes. There was nothing commonplace about this cat. He did not carry the demeanor of a broken creature but eked the pride and dignity of one born of royal blood. Like the Egyptian cat goddess, Mau, he held his head so upright and back so ramrod straight that no indignity seemed to faze him. His knowing eyes revealed that he housed an old soul, one wise beyond his years, a seer of wisdom and truth.

Eventually it happened, he began to arrive earlier and showed himself in the daylight. The coon bowls were empty and there he would sit, watching the house with that expectant look. I wanted to bang on the glass and yell, "SCAT CAT", but I was beguiled and bewitched by him. He had a power and lure about him I could not resist. My army of strays who had lined up at the window were also under his spell and seemed to be begging me to feed him. They knew that desperate feeling, for each and every one of them had experienced the misery of hunger and the fear that no one would notice.

Okay, so now we were feeding him day and night. It didn't mean a thing. We could stop any time that we wanted to. Sure we looked at him with our binoculars in the light of day, but it was just because we were curious. His beauty was absolutely crystal. We needed to find him a home before he became a sad, morbid statistic of the winter of '98.

We called neighbors, begged friends, beseeched complete strangers, even stooping to the point of approaching a K- Mart check out girl. Not one heart melted nor a single tear welled up in any eye. There was one neighborhood family that would have loved him and he them in return, but the Caesar of the household turned two thumbs down and the hopes of his subjects were dashed.

Winter temperatures waxed and waned when a frigid, near freezing, driving rain soaked the earth and Spirit Cat as well. He hovered and shivered in the cove of our covered front porch in a desperate attempt to escape the brutal elements. From time to time we would quietly crack the door and sure enough he was still there.

Next thing I knew, an impromptu kitty bed appeared on the stoop and dripping, soggy hobo lay himself down in the makeshift manger. The following evening, resourceful Ben tipped a large ceramic butter crock on its side, lined it with bedding warm from the dryer, and draped a cover over the entrance to cut the wind. Spirit Cat knew just what to do and before we went to bed we checked in on him. We reached our hands deep into the folds of the blankets and felt for the soft, silky fur of our overnight guest. Warm... for the first time in months and so sound asleep he did not even notice our intrusion. Next, an overflowing supper bowl appeared behind the crock bed and this cat, now fed and well rested, became the sentry guarding our front entrance, leaving his post only to use the facilities in the wildwood.

I began calling Spirit cat, Mr. Mustard, our little

mustard seed so filled with faith. He never doubted. His choice had been made, and it was us! On our doorstep, imbedded in the snow he left tiny paw prints, his scent was rubbed on every bush or tree in our front yard, and he took on the duty as official greeter of our entryway. He must have been thinking, "How do I get inside?"

Mother Nature said all this was very nice, but not exactly what she had in mind. So she turned down the temperatures, stirred up the old North wind and created the nastiest weather she could imagine. Oh, these poor mortals --they are so easy to manipulate. Just crank up the harsh elements of weather and those determined hearts were like putty in her hand.

All day and night the freezing wind howled flinging icy snow pellets against our windows while the shutters creaked and groaned. The ferociousness of this storm had never seen its equal. I could take no more. The worry and strain over the effects of wind-chill on animal flesh had taken its toll as I wearily headed for bed. Five minutes later Ben casually walked into the bedroom. It took a moment before I realized the purring creature embedded in the crook of his arm was a thawing Mr. Mustard, oozing with charm and beaming with contentment. The only comment from Ben's mouth was, "I guess we have another cat."

Bless his heart. We went from the traumatic struggling experience of owning six cats to now possessing seven as easily as eating cold watermelon on a hot summer day. Not one negative feeling was expressed, no heart palpitations, and positively no feeling of dread. How could this good deed possibly be wrong when it felt so perfectly right? Besides, seven is such a lucky number-- why the whole scenario seemed actually... 'Politically correct'. But for the record, I will state that I never ONCE hinted, asked, pleaded or slyly suggested that we bring this newest addition inside. It was all provider Ben's idea with a little help from those invisible forces that do get their way every now and then.

So, Spirit Cat was now a part of the in-crowd. We set him down on the floor and without hesitation he proceeded to walk through the house like he had lived there all of his life. He boldly walked up to each and every cat and they welcomed him like a long, lost brother. It was the prodigal son returning home and enjoying a most joyful reunion. The lost sheep was safely back in the fold. There was not one hiss or act of exaggerated aggression, no arched backs or bravado posturing and we stood there thoroughly in awe. Even the dogs felt as comfortable with him as if he were part of their pack. We loved it. It was pure, divine joy.

But the most amazing miracle was still to come. Mr. Mustard walked up to shell-shocked Harm and greeted him with the kindness and compassion of a dear old friend. He was the allied force that had come to rescue the prisoner of war. Mr. Mustard broke the spell of hostility that the other cats felt toward Harm and from that day forward this spirit cat took it upon himself to calm the rocky seas and heal the war-torn battle scars. Mustard tucked friend Harm under his protective wing and side-by-side they traveled the hallways and wandered the house together. Harm's transformation began immediately as he now stood up for his position at the food bowl, pushed his way into the window seat between two former enemies, and no longer cowered at the challenge of facing life.

Mr. Mustard, the Spirit Cat, changed the direction we had been heading and steered us toward more tranquil seas. He was the silver thread that bound us all together again.

Gracious and good, peacemaker and healer, spirit

guide and friend to all... Blessed Be Our Mr. Mustard.

FROM THE LAND OF CANAAN

A BIRD NAMED MOSES

The dog days of summer; sultry, long, and lazy hang heavily in the extended rays of daylight. My mind slips so easily into the summertimes of long past as I fondly hop aboard the merry-go-round of memories.

The placement for this next story was during those early years before the advent of seven cats and the lofty presence of bunnies. Our children, Ginger, Gigi, and Clint were all quite young; bustling with the excitement of grade school activities and filled with the delightful laughter and mischievous antics of youth. My days were busy with endless loads of dirty laundry, over-flowing sinks of sticky dishes and bi-weekly grocery buying expeditions that produced two heaping carts packed with multi-gallons of milk, numerous loaves of bread, and chicken noodle soup by the case. With three children of consecutive ages, a duo of dogs, one yellow parakeet named Sunshine and a husband full of vim and vinegar, life could not have seemed more complete.

I was lucky enough to be a stay-at-home mom while Ben was the band director of a local high school, so summertime gave us the luxury of three months of heavenly freedom. Monday through Friday we would give private music lessons to an endless stream of students as the house rocked with the vibrations of trumpets, trombones, tubas, and drums and rolled with the harmony of flutes, clarinets, oboes, and soulful saxophones. The workweek was busy, noisy and hectic but the weekends were reserved for nothing but fun. We tried our hand at camping and it wasn't too long before the novelty of roughing it wore off. So, we bought an adventuresome powerboat and headed for the exquisite Chain of Lakes near the border of Southern Wisconsin and Northern Illinois.

This bountiful blue craft was a grand toy and the nautical hat was jauntily worn for several seasons. We realized early on that our goal was strictly pleasure boating, as having fished once or twice, not one of us had the heart to take that snared fish from the sanctity and security of its watery home. It just seemed wrong to terminate a life for the few moments of sport, so all in unison we agreed, fishermen we were not.

Whenever the mood struck, we would arise bright and early, pack up our picnic fare and head out to that great web of water. Spread before us was a huge maze of mid-sized lakes all connected and linked by a series of natural and man-made channels that allowed passage from one body of water to the next without having to once make contact with a dry dock. It was a dream come true for anyone with an adventurous spirit or love of the water. To fulfill our need to be wild and carefree, we would spend hours speeding over the glass-like surface. The wind would tease our hair into tangled, sun bleached knots while our vessel would leapfrog over the white capped waves leaving a rolling mountain of displaced water cascading behind us. Captured by all the glory and excitement of those wide-open spaces, our hearts beat with the same velocity as the thundering motor that propelled us onward. When the untamed stallions within us had finally been satisfied, we would steer that mighty steed toward the shadowy, hushed and less frequented world that existed in the unexplored regions only accessible through the networking of channels.

Now, barely cruising at a 'no wake' pace, we found ourselves gliding between the tall marshy grasses that laced the banks of the narrow passageways and the miles of rippling lily pads flaunting their vibrant, waxy flowers. We trolled the tunnel world of lanky waterweeds and low hanging weeping willows that competed with proud cattails for the prime real estate along the waterlogged banks. It was such a contrast from the invigorating, hot, glaring sun to a cooler, laid-back time where shady oaks and dense maples produced the billowy canopy for the water flora that parted ever so effortlessly as it bowed to the presence of our boat. This was a silent, reflective time as we floated through the greenery and viewed the world through the eyes of those who called those marshes home. Our swaying craft was a voyager observing the carefully orchestrated dance between the aquatic plankton and the long legged waterfowl that stood so patiently fishing for its dinner.

This was our time to escape from pressing chores, urgent phone calls and the daily assignments that sap time and energy. At least for the day, we knew only the gentle ripple of water as it held our boat in its buoyant hand, the fine mist of a renegade wave as it sprayed our sun baked faces and the haunting cry of the seagull as it begged us to stay just a few minutes longer.

This particular outing was like so many others. Having soaked in the fun of the day, we were beginning to head toward the docking port and the relaxing drive home. Slowly moving through that final channel, we savored the last moments as the undertow current pulled our boat through the moss-hanging tree limbs. Each of us was diligently watching for a solitary waterfowl unaware of our intrusion or the glint of a school of crappies swimming by in military parade fashion.

Suddenly, something seemed wrong. Our eyes were

drawn to erratic splashing that rippled the stillness of the lily lake. It was a silent scream for help, an urgent plea to draw attention to the terrifying struggle of that pivotal point between life and death. Ben steered the bow of the boat toward the frantic commotion so we could get a closer look.

There in the center of the splashing was a soggy, drowning, mass of soaked feathers. Its wings were extended as in flight but now were being used as buoys to try to keep the frightened, beaked face from succumbing to a suffocating watery demise. With only a few minutes of fight left in this severely exhausted swimmer, the panic of the situation registered in its wide-eyed look and gaping mouth. We grabbed our never used fishing net and reached over the side to scoop this grotesquely tangled, matted lump of wings and kicking legs from the brink of its Waterloo. This glob of soaked plumage was placed on the bottom of the boat as we tried to determine just exactly what it was. Lying there, heaving from complete exhaustion while coughing up the water that had been choking its airways, it shivered and convulsed from the sheer horror of being the victim of such a ghastly experience.

Our hearts ached when we realized the new passenger was a tiny wisp of a baby bird. It was not a duck or crane infant that was naturally drawn to water, but a land dweller, a tree hugger, a dry earth inhabitant. Upon examining the nearly dead victim, we noticed the slightest hint of color in the disarray of feathers on his water-soaked chest. They were distinctly orange. This was a baby robin. From the pool of water that had drained from his body, a wobbly, weak head looked up and thanked us profusely for saving his life. He had been just seconds away from a terrible death and there was no way those soggy wings could have broken free from the heavy grip of clinging seaweed that had intended to drag its victim into the watery abyss.

More than likely this was his premiere flight and being so filled with inexperienced exuberance he headed out to see what that great expanse of sun-rippled splendor might be. Because of his youth, he had no knowledge of impending danger or the peril of the sea. Nor could the call of alarm from his mother deter him from an overconfident zest to explore the open spaces and unobstructed glory of this exciting new world. His baby wings did not have the strength to return him to the green leafed arms of his birth tree and security of the home nest, so he decided the glossy, flat field of lily pads seemed like a perfect landing strip for a slalom air skier. But those circular plates of waxy green were only capable of supporting the weight of a curious frog or resting dragonfly and this clumsily landing baby bird careened into the briny brink.

However it happened, what we had now was a tired, cold, and downed pilot whose very life depended upon us. We scanned the tree-lined banks searching the shadow woods for that traditional orange breast of his mother and carefully listened for the distinctive chirp of a frantic parent overcome with distress and despair. Fifteen, twenty, thirty minutes passed before we realized there was never going to be a mother and child reunion. The connection had been broken, the lifeline disconnected, this wayfarer was now a homeless waif. All that could be done was bundle our new infant in a fuzzy, terry cloth towel, hold him close for comforting warmth and head homeward in a direction many miles away.

He was appropriately christened 'Moses' after the Biblical leader, for he too was drawn out of the water and rescued from the tangled tentacles of bulrush. We never doubted the gentle nudge that guided our chance meeting, for clearly this was not the day intended that this baby robin should perish.

Moses slept in his swaddling cloth all the way home and we gave him the luxury of undisturbed, restful quiet only peeking in on him occasionally to make sure he still numbered among the living. He was so bone tired from the sheer exhaustion of such immense physical exercise that all of his muscles limply lay in double-jointed configurations. He showed no display of emotion, only that naive trusting spirit that somehow we knew what we were doing. But in reality, we had no knowledge of what would be necessary to maintain his survival. Could he ever adjust to people or would he forever be in an overwhelming state of fear and panic at the mere sight of us? Would his life with us be more hazardous then that watery crypt that he had just escaped from?

Finally home, a call to our vet friend was the first order of business. He came right over and with the confident touch of a healer he began to examine our now only slightly damp nester. Vet Deere carefully checked for wounds, BB shot, broken bones or mangled wings. He probed the belly then rib cage for signs of internal damage and looked deep into the eyes and nose of the well-behaved patient. Everything was fine, actually the newcomer was in excellent shape and the only pressing need was his tremendous appetite.

The orders began to fly, "Get me a can of dog food, an eye dropper, Carnation evaporated milk, and also a toothpick." With a flurry of activity, we responded with mach speed. Doc Deere informed us that baby birds perish quickly from lack of nutrition and it had been many hours since the last feeding. He expertly held our little Moses in one hand and with the toothpick in the other; he pried the still-soft side edge of his beak open while Ben, ready with a tiny bite of dog food waited for his cue. In split second timing the beak was open, the food dropped in, and the recognition of nourishment registered on one hungry bird face. Mission accomplished! Two more bites, a dropper full of milk and Moses was back in slumber land. Dr. Deere declared, "This bird will live. Congratulations, you are the new parents of a bouncing baby boy."

At first, we would pry Moses' mouth open every time to feed him, but before long he caught on to our task, and responded with a wide-open beak and urgent chirping for more and more food.

Our family felt the tremendous responsibility of raising this tiny bird to adulthood as each of us was dedicated to the demanding and time consuming job. Doc Deere's advice to most clients was to let the baby bird that had 'fallen' from the nest remain where it had landed, for the mother bird was always near by and she was the best one to take care of her own offspring. He bemoaned the fact that many people bring in infant birds, bunnies, squirrels, and other young wild life that eventually die, even in his expert care, but could have survived if they had just been left alone. "Nature has its own course and when humans intervene, many times it just ends in disaster," he would sadly say.

But he did concede, that in our case divine intervention thrust the situation upon us and we had done the noble and correct thing by bringing him home. On his way out the door Dr. Deere reminded us that being foster parents would change our footloose, carefree life style and that we would forever more admire the work mother birds do to raise their young.

How right he was! Moses was a bottomless pit when it came to nourishment. Every two hours he demanded his dog food and was constantly on the look out for someone to feed him. Once spotted, his mouth would fly open while chirping and cheeping in the most demanding tones. Of course, with this chowhound needing attention every few hours, our family was more housebound than ever. Plans were cancelled that might make us late for mid-day feedings and we left early from picnics and gatherings to go home and care for baby Moses. Eventually we just packed up bird, cage, and food supplies and took Moses on the road with us. He didn't mind, he was a trooper and his great love of exploring had already been documented, so our family of five became a clan of six. We took Moses everywhere, on Sunday drives, antique shopping in Galena and even back to his old stomping ground on the lake for a day of surf and sun.

Oh, how blessed our family was to have that baby robin. When finally dried out and fluffed up he was extremely beautiful. His feathers were all a downy, speckled brown that surrounded an orange chest the exact color of a pale amber evening sunset. He was gangly and clumsy while being filled with an unquenchable curiosity that gave us an insight into his excellent intelligence. So typical of all robins, Moses would never look straight down on the object of his intent but turn his head in a cockeyed angle and peer at it with the eye closest to it. The crooking of his head made him seem like a very deep thinker and he could spend endless hours playing with paper clips, bits of string, and anything bright and shiny. Such a wonderful temperament in this baby bird. He was playful, affectionate, and simply bursting with a love of life.

Having Moses as a close member of our family, we had the privilege of touching a part of the wild kingdom that most can only observe from afar. His bony, long legs with their multi-jointed toes would curl around our fingers as he held on to us for dear life when we transported him around the house. He would peck ever so gently at our skin, tussle our hair and explore the folds of our clothes in an endless search for something more to eat. He loved us-- he truly did. It was as though he had forgotten all that was his past and accepted everything in his present with not the slightest question or concern. He definitely was part of the family and living indoors with people, dogs, and a golden parakeet suited him just fine.

Moses displayed as much personality as any domesticated pet, a clown in feathers who charmed us into realizing that birds were as sweet and good-natured as any puppy or kitten. How could we have possibly known those seemingly endless flocks that decorated our skies all possessed personality traits very much like our own? We had always just assumed they were a dull, mindless, busy swarm robotically attending to their lives with no feelings of love, humor or sorrow. But Moses had taught us differently. It was as though a veil had been lifted and he wanted us to come to the realization that all creatures; wild, domestic and human were really very much alike, all brothers under the skin.

Moses grew quickly and matured into a stunningly handsome male robin. He was surprisingly large for his species, (could it have been all that dog food?). He loved to ride around the house on our shoulders and play on the bed with our children, as only children know how. It all seemed so natural to keep a wild bird inside.

We were so taken with him and he appeared perfectly content, but there was that haunting feeling in our hearts that deep down inside something was missing. Born wild, he needed to be free. We wanted him to have a mate, family, and most of all wanted him to fly. Not just the short flights from the cage to the top of our heads, but those long and lofty climbs to the treetops and then the gala swoop downward floating on the fingertips of the wind.

Ben and I sat the children down to tell them of our resolution. Moses deserved more than what we could offer and although he was our special gift for a short time, he needed to be returned to his intended environment. They were upset about losing their new playmate but accepted our decision with an understanding coming from something deeper than their youthful intelligence. It was wisdom drawn from the ages, an inborn knowledge of the persistent call of the wild and powerful pressure propelling the survival of the species.

So, aeronautical training was stage one of operation *bird-launch*. Flight instructor Ben took this job upon his shoulders and with the dedication of a drill sergeant, doled out the necessary exercises to strengthen those unsteady wings and wimpy landing attempts. Hut two, three, four. The kids and I would sit on the couch like the reviewing stand while Moses would go through his paces. Ben would put the eager recruit on his hand and move him up and down from ceiling to floor. Each time this exercise became progressively faster causing Moses to extend his wings to keep his balance and also experience the thrust and resistance of wind velocity. Eventually the hand would pull away and free falling Moses had to sink or swim (figuratively speaking). There were many belly flops and nosedive landings but Moses was always game to get back on that jump tower and try again. He was full of spunk, courageous as a lion and a flier with the guts of the best top gun pilot.

His flying skills were perfected rather quickly, as he seemed to relish that part of the training even if he wasn't much for landings. He smashed into windows, overshot objects as broad as the couch, slid off countertops, and bounced off tables and chairs while eventually ending up on the floor. It was nothing less than a miracle that we could endure watching him tumble and fall after raising him so tenderly and yet we realized he had to learn-- and landing on carpeting did soften the blow some.

Finally the day arrived when Moses was ready to go outside and take that great flight into the sky. It was a huge family event as we all envisioned him soaring into the heavens and bidding us adieu. Freedom... that magical word we imagined he must have longed for.

Ben held him high above his head and we all held our breath as we waited for the great lift off. Moses did look around some, but he just held on all the tighter to his daddy's finger. He did not want to leave, he was already home and besides he was wondering, "Wasn't it about time to eat"? Our minds raced with questions. What were we going to do now? Was it legal to keep a wild bird? Would it be ethically correct?

We did not want to push Moses into something he was not ready for, so we began by taking his cage outside during the day and letting him acclimate to this new environment. Mostly he would sit there watching the house waiting for someone to come outside to feed him his next meal. If we were busy doing yard work or the kids were playing, then he would perk up and participate. His favorite activities were sitting on Ben's shoulder while he mowed the lawn, landing on the heads of the children as they ran through the sprinkler, chasing ants and riding the backs of the dogs like a rodeo stunt rider. It was all taken in such a playful spirit with each adventure more fun than the one before. He did notice the other birds that were flying over head and landing in the trees above him, but he preferred walking over flying, and when he was in a hurry he would break into a full fledged run.

At nighttime we always brought him inside as danger was lurking for a young bird that chose a yard chair as his highest peak. Eventually Moses began to pick at the food bowl and no longer needed our help for nourishment. Curiosity led him to try his wings on his own. We found him doing the silliest things. We couldn't help but laugh, as he looked so out of place on the top of the car, holding on to the roof gutters or peeking out from the center of a small tree.

Then one day we saw him take a huge soaring flight out of sight, circling around the neighbor's yard and peering down at us from high above. How little we must have looked to him. He began to spend longer and longer times away from our yard and then one day we realized he brought his new friends home with him. From the average observer it just looked like a flock of identical looking birds, all robins with the same markings and mannerisms, but to the parents of that most amazing bird, we knew exactly which one was our foster child. He was the one who overshot the landing strip and bumped into the edge on the patio fence, skidding to an abrupt, topsy-turvy stop. That was our Moses all right!

We had such mixed feelings about his new life. Each of us missed the daily interaction and seeing his funny face peering at us from around the corner of our kitchen. Yet we were happy that he was now in his natural environment with a flock of contemporaries. Little did we realize that years later when our own children left the nest we would feel the exact same emotions.

There was no final farewell, no great fanfare or heartfelt sendoff. Moses just gradually severed the ties that bound us together. We hoped he was still nearby and occasionally he might fly over and bid us a fond hello. Sometimes our hearts longed for the feeling of having him land on the top of our heads for that bumpy ride he liked so well. Moses opened the door for many orphaned birds that followed him. The story of the family that raised baby birds spread like wildfire and scores of people sought us out to save the underdeveloped foundlings that they had rescued. Soon I was known by the neighborhood children as *the bird lady.* Our kitchen counter was filled with multiple cages mixing the species like M&M's in a candy bowl. Sparrows bunked with blue jays and starlings broke bread with crows. The adage, "birds of a feather flock together" did not apply at our hotel, for all breeds mixed and mingled as no difference of color or size entered into the equation. It was our little piece of a multicultural heaven, a peek into what perfect harmony could be.

Sometimes when musing with family and friends I like to ask, "What activity do you most want to do when you get to heaven?" The answers were well thought through and as diversified as the people who responded. One wanted to be a historian, another the caregiver of babies, many wished to sing in the angelic choir or fill the heavens with the mellow golden sound of the guitar. There were those who felt the need to teach and some who were drawn to the tending of the flowers and even one who wanted to create magnificent stained glass windows for that house not built with human hands.

As for Ben and myself, well, we are going to take care of the downtrodden animals. Those bony, shaggy, mangy strays that never knew a gentle word or kind stroke, the sadly abused that lived a lifetime chained to a stake or cruelly imprisoned in a cage and whose only contact with humans filled them with trembling fear and constant pain. And of course, look after all those that we had the privilege to raise and love.

When that day arrives and I am standing there in paradise, I won't be surprised when a lovely, male robin comes soaring from above and clumsily lands on the top of my head. I will know that Moses has come home. He will tell me about all of his adventures while sharing stories of mate and offspring. What a glorious reunion it will be. Our little Moses, rescued from the water, conqueror of the sky, and a fine-feathered fellow will be perched upon my shoulder for eternity.

WHEELER, MY KINDRED SPIRIT

Life and literature seem to portray parallel universes when they chronicle the stories of nature's most unfortunate victims. The Classics established the ground rules for observing the prime examples of how mankind nobly adjusts or is harshly broken by the physical or emotional limitations that fate has bestowed upon them.

There is a sense of villainy in those characters that strike out with hostility and belligerence toward the society they punish for their burdens. Frankenstein and Mr. Hyde both sought out murder and mayhem as their equalizer in a world where they only felt rejection and scorn. The Phantom of the Opera chose to physically retreat yet still make his presence known through his covert acts of sinister rage. The grotesquely deformed Quasimodo in Victor Hugo's *Hunchback of Notre Dame* did not retaliate for his banishment from society but reacted to his role as outcast by cowering with shame and embarrassment. Only when he was taunted and tortured did he express his frustration through violence and anger.

But not all victims of tragic circumstances are frighteningly evil or pitifully shattered. There is much admiration for Dickens's ailing Tiny Tim, burdened with his crippled leg yet beaming with a loving, forgiving temperament. Readers felt the tug of their heartstrings at the mere prospect of his little chair sitting empty and a Christmas dinner without his cheery outlook on life. The sweet, gentle invalid, Beth, of *Little Women* displayed her unselfish virtue and true caring nature by never disclosing any animosity in spite of the doomed, inescapable destiny that was to be her ultimate demise. Jane Eyre, the painfully shy, emotionally battered governess who struggled a lifetime with her own demons of low self-esteem was kept isolated by self-doubt until she realized she could comfort one more miserable than she. These are just a few of the fictional personalities in the literary world that found acceptance of life despite adversity and those held in high admiration for their strength of character and pure intentions.

True life is often more remarkable than fiction. Helen Keller, the world's most admired person, displayed remarkable courage while facing a multitude of formidable obstacles. This woman inspired us all to try harder to overcome challenges as she faced darkness, silence, and isolation with an attitude that was never defeated or discouraged. We have been blessed with blind musicians, Ray Charles and Stevie Wonder, who have demonstrated that sight is not a necessity when reaching deep into the musical soul. Genius scientist Steven Hawkings, held prisoner by a most crippling disease and yet looking ever forward to uncover the secrets of the universe chose not to be held hostage by his fate. So, understandably we are drawn by a sense of admiration to those individuals, who when faced with devastating tribulations do not strike out with anger or hate but find optimism and benevolence as their solution.

Thus it was with our little gray-striped, tiger cat named Wheeler. His life began with the tremendous disadvantage of chronic disease, progressed through abandonment and over-whelming sorrow to continue with disillusioning bewilderment. All were heaped unfairly upon this infant kitten and yet his indomitable spirit, so filled with optimism and hope, could not be broken by cruel fate. He would not let it change his direction and outlook on life. He would not bow to defeat. Wheeler is one of the unsung heroes of the animal world and I feel quite honored to tell the story of our Little Wheely Wheeler.

Most multi-pet owners can never choose just one pet as their favorite. They are all so individual, special and unique in their own particular ways. One may be more out-going and always there to greet you at the front door, while another more affectionate and your nightly TV lapmate. Still another with the ability to bring comfort on an especially sad day can lift your spirits as no other can. They become spokes in the wheel of your life and each holds their own special gift. It is virtually impossible to separate all the levels of pure love and devotion for these beings giving their full measure without judgment, bias or prejudice.

But for this chapter, I have chosen to tell the story of Wheeler for he is a very special presence and indeed a shining star that twinkles just a bit brighter because of his adversity. I call him my 'animal soul mate', a kindred spirit that peers so deeply into my soul he relays to me, "I have known you always."

Wheeler was born into a world that did not want him, an unplanned birth that was a burden, a hindrance, and one huge inconvenience. His mother was a sickly cat plagued with a respiratory disease that so stressed her system, pregnancy would have seemed impossible. But nature's one-track mind is obsessive about the survival of the species and even though her body was wracked with infirmity, the reproductive system was unaffected and still quite fertile. Three malnourished, unhealthy kittens doomed with the same affliction were the result placed upon a society encumbered with the problem of dealing with the overpopulation of homeless animals.

The human that discovered the nest of baby kittens wanted no part of them. He did not even want to wait until they were weaned and had at least a fighting chance of survival. Certainly there was no effort to find them a home, just the pressing need to dispose of them as he took the tiny helpless kittens and dumped them along a lonely stretch of rural highway without a farmhouse or sign of humanity in sight. If left singly alone, each surely would have perished, but the three of them united in a cause that gave courage and hope to one another. This little family consisted of two females and one male, all gray-striped, stunted in growth and desperately in need of their mother's nourishing milk.

There were two options that loomed ahead for them that day. One was to remain where they had been dumped and ultimately succumb to death by starvation or take the other choice and begin the tedious journey— one paw placed ahead of the other in search of their salvation. A towering cornfield, miles long, acres wide and well into its full height was the primeval forest directly in their path. They entered into this unknown territory not knowing whether it would lead to survival or be the place where they would collapse, too weak to continue and ultimately become a meal to the ever-searching scavengers who prey upon the young and helpless.

The journey of a million steps began that early dawn and ended three grueling days later. Our country friends, Jan, Darwin and daughter Amy lived in the farmhouse on the far side of this acreage and were besieged for seventy-two heart-wrenching hours by the constant meowing from the three panicked kittens. These abandoned babies were so hysterical with fear; not one minute did they stop their frantic wailing. A trio of voices pleading for help, verbalizing their despair while remaining close together as they encouraged one another to just keep advancing forward.

Those pitiful wails would have broken their dear mother's heart and the family in the big white farmhouse worried about the outcome of the three lost kittens. To search the dense field would have been impossible, so all they could do was wait and hope by some miracle they would emerge and find the solace of their sprawling front porch already inhabited by some fifteen to twenty stray cats.

As the threesome finally cleared that humongous cornfield, their eyes squinted at the fierce summer sun. It had been a continuous fight of trekking through the parched soil while razor-sharp corn stalks sliced their faces and paws. But even though brutally tough on the young trailblazers, the first major obstacle in their lives had been overcome and they triumphed victorious. Thirst, hunger and tattered fur were now forgotten as they realized what lay ahead of them. It was the vision of Oz... the lovely white two-story structure with a wraparound porch, the compassion of humans and the delectable odor of food. The anxious kittens, weakened and fatigued, were enthralled by their good fortune. There was a pot of gold at the end of their rainbow and the vagabonds rejoiced at their good luck.

But between them and the land of plenty was an obstacle they had never encountered before. Lying ahead was a blacktop roadway, not particularly massive but wrought with its own set of dangers. It manifested itself as cold and hard but days of baking in the scorching relentless sun had boiled it until ripples of hot air seemed to sizzle off of its surface. It appeared that their next obstacle was to be a trial by fire.

The two sisters and little brother had rested long enough as the land of glory was just a matter of yards ahead of them. Older sister took the lead for she was first born and her spirit was one of confidence and daring. Brave, bold and fearless were the characteristics that directed this natural born leader as she darted across the hot, tarry roadway with no hesitation or fear of this new situation. Once on the opposite side she looked back to call the others onward. Her meows relayed to the remaining two that the black river was not so ominous, somewhat hot to tender feet but the burns were not searing or permanent.

Baby brother Wheely was next to venture across. With one sister in front and one behind, their encouragement surrounded the airwaves, each one meowing loudly to shore up his courage. Eyes straight ahead, holding tail upright, walking as if on a tight rope, he placed one paw straight in front of the other with his eyes ever on the goal. The soft, cool grass and the sweet scent of older sister were a wonderful reward for his bravery. Finally on the safe gravel, his heart stopped racing and he could take a long needed breath of fresh air. What a joyful reunion for brother and sister as they greeted one another on the freedom side of the black river.

Now to complete the circle. They beckoned middle sister to join them and then all together they would collect their prize. Middle sister looked so little, forlorn and much too tiny to be left all alone. She trembled in fear for she did not possess the explorer spirit of older sister or the have the blind confidence of younger brother. She was plagued with self-doubts about her ability to muster the courage to face the great unknown by herself. Identical girl kittens, yet one so bold and self-assured and one so very hesitant and meek. What inner voices whispered to one to face life squarely and then to the other to cower from the challenge?

Brother and sister called and called. "It is safe. Cross now and join us in the Promised Land." Middle sister started across, slower and less confident then either one before her and then she suddenly stopped midway...

frozen in fear. She was incapable of making the decision to dart ahead or run back to the safety of the cornfield, as coming straight toward her was a monstrous black form. It made only the slightest noise, just a mechanical sound of valves and pistons cranking out a rhythm as it harmonized with the hum of spinning tires that promised destruction to anything that got in its way. It appeared steely cold and heartless with two glassy eyes and a smirking chrome smile that seemed to mock her vulnerable predicament. Why should this impending monster care about an insignificant kitten, a tiny helpless life that had already known too much heartache and suffering, who needed just a few more moments to complete the blacktop obstacle and gather the laurels of the win.

Perhaps neither the car nor driver realized that tiny bump in the road was the ending of her young life. The only witnesses to this fateful happening were two horrified siblings and a heaven full of angels. One second an infant soul so filled with high hopes and exciting aspirations and the next moment just a lifeless battered shell, crushed bones and shattered dreams.

To some it was only a dead kitten laying in the roadway, just another carcass that eventually would be pulverized into the dust, but to Wheeler and his sister the shocking episode stopped their world. How could this have happened? Together they had survived the gamble of birth, the premature separation from their mother, the disillusionment of indifference, and the obstacle of the brutal cornfield to emerge still together into the hopeful daylight. And now the blade of the grim reaper had cruelly separated the trio for the simple mistake of a moment of hesitation. Why was this kitten killed now? Was there to be no reward for her struggle, her courage, all that she had suffered?

The lifeless, limp body of middle sister did not respond to her sibling's plaintive cries and it wasn't until the dry summer breeze sent the smell of death in their direction that they truly realized the finality of her life. It seems all animals understand the odor of a body no longer governed by a soul and so the two remaining kittens turned away from their sister and silently walked through the yard that led to the homestead. The army of stray cats that resided on the porch moved from their path and let the two shell-shocked infants pass without the normal greetings that newcomers usually face. These refugees numbly made their way to the food dish and filled their painfully empty stomachs but there was no joy in their journey's end, only the haunted look of disillusioned eyes.

Wheeler and older sister were gently welcomed into the sanctuary of our country friends and received immediate care and attention. Jan later recalled to us that these were the two tiniest kittens they had ever seen away from their mother and marveled they had survived their merciless ordeal.

But at least Wheeler and older sister still had each other and bonded even more closely, never straying more than a hair's breath apart. Country daughter Amy was the first to notice the congested condition both young cats seemed plagued with. After consulting a vet, medicine was administered for a condition that should not have been present in babies so young. Mother's milk with its natural immunization usually protected newborns from this ailment, but after the treatment showed no improvement, it was deduced that their upper-respiratory disease had been passed from infected mother to kittens and they also would suffer their lifetime battling this suffocating struggle for air. It was a condition plagued with symptoms of having a constant head cold, draining eyes, plugged yet runny nose and the blockage of swollen mucus membranes robbing the luxury of ever taking a complete breath. The victims had a wheezing, noisy breathing kind of characteristic, much like a toddler who hadn't learned the trick of blowing or wiping the annoyance away.

Because of this disease, these two kittens lost the capacity of the surprise attack, which is the cat's greatest advantage over their prey. This malady took away their most valuable hunting ploy, the silence of the stalker. Wheeler and older sister could be heard thirty feet away and no field mouse or chipmunk would ever be ambushed by this duo of rolling thunder.

In the safe haven of the porch, they had food, shelter and complete acceptance into the cat colony. Under the care of kind humans, life was finally free of stressful strife and the kittens began to grow and mature. But the many days of ravaging starvation had affected their development and may have likely contributed to their unhealthy nature and tiny frames.

All the established cats that lived on the porch understood about 'The Dogs'. It was a live and let live society, no real friendships between species, but neither viewed the other as mortal enemies either. The cats basically had the front porch, side yard and all the fields surrounding the farm. The dogs took the back porch, driveway, and made their rounds between the farm buildings and horse corrals. There had been a few squabbles, but neither feline nor canine seemed to be looking for a fight or confrontation and like the relationships on most farms, tolerance and acceptance were the norm.

It was a day that started with no hint of foreboding or gloom. Wheeler and older sister were headed off to the large horse barn for a day of mousing. The other cats on the front porch were glad they were gone for it was impossible to get a decent nap with the constant rumbling of their noisy breathing. Off to catch a mouse or maybe just an afternoon of hide and seek was anticipated as the two little siblings snuffed and sniffled across the spacious drive.

Laying in the shade of the back porch, the head honcho Rottweiler had never before taken notice of the newest arrivals. Cats were usually no big deal to him, but these two were so irritating and different that his curiosity got the best of him and he felt compelled to check them out. So typical of his breed he had a face as big as a black bear, hulking, muscular shoulders and a body with the fitness tone of a professional wrestler. His presence was powerful, massive, and unstoppable. As he approached them, the kittens tried to discern what he reminded them of. When the memory finally registered, the reality was terrifying. He appeared identical to that huge black shadow that had killed middle sister and immobilized by fear they watched him steadily approach with that same dogged determination, closer and closer looming ever larger.

Older sister was like a survivor who had helplessly witnessed the Holocaust atrocities and pledged a vow to never be a passive victim again. She realized her slight body was the only shield that stood between the oncoming destructive force and her baby brother as this tiny soldier took her stand by blocking a trembling Wheeler from the approaching heinous beast. Hair raised, back arched, claws unsheathed and a voice that snarled her protective intentions were her only weapons. She had not been able to save her sister, but this time she would do battle to protect her only remaining family member. The dog bound up, only curious for a quick sniff and then on his way. What he encountered was a wild, fearless attack tigress who leaped up into the air and on the way down targeted the mug and tender nose as the place to inflict the most damage. Razor edged claws embedded in very sensitive flesh and ripped downward with the body weight of the hissing assailant.

Wheeler watched in stunned horror at the actions and reactions of a hostile universe that seemed to play in slow motion to his disbelieving mind. The battle cry and attack of his brave sister, the howl from the dog monster that abruptly turned into a snarl, the gnash of powerful teeth, the scream of pain and the gurgle of death. It all happened so quickly, a fatal mistake and the instantaneous deathblow that followed. The dog, hardly aware of what he had done returned to the back porch to nurse his slivered nose and Wheeler raced over to the mutilated, quivering, broken body of one who sacrificed her own life to save his.

Poor Wheely, overcome with despair, lay across the cooling carcass of his adored sister trying to comfort and stop the spilling of her life-blood. When he sensed her soul had left, he gave up all hope and relinquished his own will to live. This phenomenon is well documented in human tragedies and often told about in the animal kingdom as well. A heart so overcome with grief it rejects the life force within and chooses to step over the threshold and join the deceased in the land of the dead. Wheeler would have united with both sisters that very day if not for the intervention of a wise old cat that had watched the entire episode. This sage of wisdom left the sanctity of the porch and approached the limp, fading spirit of young Wheeler and communicated in a language humans have no knowledge of. He relayed to the despondent youngster it was not yet his time and that his mission here on earth had not been fulfilled. Then the old cat drew Wheeler back into the land of the living and gently escorted him to the shelter of the porch. Wheeler climbed up upon that wicker chair he and older sister had shared and took comfort in her scent as it slowly faded while the days melted into weeks.

What sad and terrible memories must be stored in the psyche of that little innocent cat? What bleak nightmares must he face when sleep overcomes him? What part of his broken heart is still oozing with grief and despair?

No one would have been surprised if Wheeler had changed into a timid, skittish, frightened cat for these many strikes against him would have disillusioned even the most buoyant of personalities. But his indomitable spirit was not to be destroyed by all this tragedy, sadness or illness. Wheeler grew into adult cat hood in the tender care of the country family, who understood the melancholy of his past and watched as this funny little valentine of a character became a greeter of people who, despite his most frightful experience actually liked dogs.

It was early October when we stopped by the farm for a visit and also with a mission in mind. Daughter, Gigi, had approached us with the prospect of adding a cat to her household and Jan had invited us out to find one that would fit her requirements. What an overwhelming decision we were faced with. All ages, colors and descriptions of cats greeted us on that crisp fall afternoon. We were the center of attraction with purring felines all vying for our attention.

Then Ben noticed a lone gray tiger sitting on a wicker chair on the far side of the sprawling porch. Something about that wise little face drew them together and within minutes the decision was made, Wheeler was going home with us. Jan commented that Wheely was Darwin's favorite of all the cats, explained his health problems, told us the story of his sad past and gave her blessing to our union.

So now this country boy was to become a city dweller, an outside hunter was to become an inside playboy. His adjustment was quite easy and when those blustery winds and foot high snows covered the earth, Wheeler was more than happy to walk on soft carpet and burrow into the warm center of a toasty afghan. We brought Wheeler to several vets hoping to find a cure to relieve him of his distress and because of that he suffered through a grueling siege of pills, nose drops, shots and medications. Finally we realized nothing was going to help. The most we had to offer was tender loving care. We decided to keep him for ourselves because of his medical history and also because we grew to love him so.

Wheely, sometimes called Wheezy, is more work than any of the other cats. He constantly needs the dried matter from his eyes scraped away, his nose mopped and a major clean up when he lets loose with one of his huge sneezes. When his congestion gets so bad he seems close to suffocation from blocked mucus we bring him into the bathroom and run the shower with hot steamy water. That Swedish sauna-like atmosphere gives him some relief and in the foggy haze he seems to sense the medicinal benefits and practices deep breathing exercises. He comes out feeling much better and also appears all puffed-up with a kinky little curl in his usually straight hair.

Even with all of his respiratory distress we never get any complaints from him. He plays hard with the other cats, is the best sleep buddy to the bunnies, and shares in the fun of upstairs-downstairs hide and seek. He nightly washes the huge face of Bubba, and basically is the best adjusted of all our cats.

Wheely is our *wise man* when it comes to the character of people. He takes it upon himself to welcome everyone who enters our house and is loved by all. But there have been a select few who rejected him and were irritated by his affectionate advances. Ben and I have always believed how people feel about animals seems to define a very important part of their personality and a red flag of caution rises toward those who spurn Wheely's friendship. Over the years, in our role as parents, we have told our children when entering the dating world in search of the perfect mate to stay clear of anyone who professes no affection for animals. If their newly intended can not find love in their heart for an innocent, loving animal, then how could they possibly have any real feelings for a human being so filled with flaws and foibles? We have concluded there is just something missing in the temperament of a person who does not hold any compassion for animals.

We have been advised that cats will only eat when motivated by their sense of smell. Several vets have warned us that if Wheeler's condition should get worse, he could completely lose his ability to distinguish food, stop eating and become seriously ill. So to ensure that Wheeler eats well every day he is bestowed with his own saucer of 'kitty stew' each morning and this stinky little gourmet meal keeps him healthy, frisky and raring to go.

Many animal behaviorists seem to believe that those who reside in the animal kingdom are incapable of deductive reasoning. They profess there is no evidence that any species other than man has the intelligence to think, plot, scheme or reason beyond pure animal instinct. I would love to introduce them to our amazing Wheeler who is wise, cunning, and possibly the Einstein of the feline universe.

Wheeler loves to sleep with us at night in our bedroom. Just tuck him under an arm, cover him with the comforter and he does not move a muscle until the alarm goes off in the morning. The only problem is that his breathing is so noisy all the other occupants in the room are kept wide-awake while he snores and rattles in slumbering bliss.

After several nights of this Evinrude motor running in our ears, we came to the conclusion that one of us was going to have to exit the bedroom at night. All fingers pointed to little Wheezy; the noisemaker had to go.

For weeks he would meow at the closed bedroom door begging then demanding entrance. Finally he abandoned that approach and began planning his next strategy. We would often watch the late evening news while preparing for bed, door open with cats or dogs entering and leaving at will. But when the sports came on, the set went off, cats escorted out and door closed. Then lights turned off, soothing quiet and finally sleep.

Little did we realize that there was a stowaway hiding under a dresser. In the tomb-like silence was a small boned, gray-striped visitor who by controlling his rattling breathing possessed the knowledge that his ever present snuffing would have given away his secret presence. Tiny, shallow, noiseless breaths were coming from a cat that had never known a silent moment in his life. When we had fallen sound asleep, then and only then would a very smart and conniving Wheeler gently jump up on the bed, head for a soft clump of covers and proceed to sleep where he deemed his rightful place to be. He is wise enough to change his hiding spot every night and his superior intelligence has outsmarted us more times than we like to admit.

He pulls the same stunt with Pumpkin who does not particularly want a noisy sleep mate either. So Wheely waits until the big, overstuffed melon-colored feline is securely in slumber land and then proceeds to work himself into the half moon curl of his somewhat plumpish cat brother. There is no wonder why Wheeler is so content... his sleeping place is warm, soft and purring. I can't imagine how he came up with the idea, but Wheeler's philosophy is that 'everyone should own an orange cat.'

Wheely is truly our dear sweet child. He is Ben's bathroom buddy as he watches him get ready for work every morning, my helpmate trudging through the household chores, the fearless explorer of the empty grocery bags, best friend to all cats, dogs, bunnies and birds, and welcoming committee to our friends and family. Wheeler is one who refuses to be pulled down by the millstones of his tragic past but radiates in the ever-hopeful promise of the future. He is our Tiny Tim, the spirit of good will, who truly believes in the simple message, 'God Bless Us Everyone.'

OUR BOY RUSTY

THE GENTLE GIANT WITH A GOLDEN HEART

It has been well over a year since the first word of *Pawprints Upon My Heart* was placed upon the page and what an evolution it has been. The tulip bulb long buried within the mud has pushed and prodded through the thick, dry, crusty soil to rupture mother earth and finally get a glimpse of the sunshine that it knew lay just out of reach. Once free of the bonds of confinement, the pale, tender sprout could not be stopped from reaching, stretching, and yearning for all that the sunbeam promised.

The stem brought forth the leaves that untucked the sheltered bud as it pushed higher and higher toward the pastel blue heavens. An apprehensive sheathed flower, shy at what it might face, opened tentatively-- curious about what it would encounter in a world it was seeing for the very first time. This awaking was the genesis for intertwining dreams of the past and hopes of the future. Beaming in earnest, this persona of petals faced the unforeseen. Always cognizant of its origin, the flower head bowed in sincere respect to the maternal bulb from which its wellspring of life originated. This finally mature blossom joyfully disclosed innermost thoughts and shared emotions that had long been slumbering in the safety of the seed.

Now, Pawprints is at the crossroads of the final chapter; and I am searching for closing thoughts and then a sad fare-thee-well, for this correspondence has come to the end of the garden tour. I fondly embrace the metaphor of comparing the journey of this manuscript to the yearly passing of the seasons.

The birth of these stories had the youthfulness of spring, a time so fresh and exciting that the joy of writing purely leaped from the pen onto the paper. I felt consumed with boundless energy and an uncontrollable thirst to experience the new, uncharted territories of my mind.

As the stories progressed into the more stabilizing demeanor of the summer phase, there was an endless search for variety in embellishment while striving to capture the rhythm and rhyme as one traverses the stepping-stones from thought to thought. Like the hot sweltering midday sun, my enthusiasm was recharged by the awesome power of abstract ideas being transposed from a vision into words.

As the natural flow ebbed, a more calm and complacent attitude developed, thus the autumn passages were written. A time of harvesting mature emotions driven by a need to pass along a bit of philosophy as to what our purpose and obligations should be to endow a better world for the animal future. It was a time to feel the grace of spirit as it ignited inner peace recaptured by telling the tales of those that had passed over to a more perfect place.

And now, Pawprints is sensing a change in the direction of its seasons-- its winter is approaching as this final chapter gently draws to a bittersweet conclusion. My wonderful journey has now become complete and it is time to tuck away the quill and ink, prepare to crawl under the downy quilts and dream of the next adventure that might cross my path.

Faced with the insurmountable task of choosing the subject for the last chapter, it was difficult to decide which of the multitude of remaining pets should be featured before the curtain was drawn for the final time. Amidst the confusion of a mind overflowing with stewing and brooding, there seemed to be no perfect conclusion. In utter frustration, this dilemma was voiced to son, Clint, and he seemed surprised at my indecision. With not the slightest hesitation it was undoubtedly crystal clear to him. "Why it should be Rusty, of course!" The last piece of the puzzle had just been snapped ever so perfectly into place.

Rusty was the most gentle, loving, friendly, ambassador of good will to have ever set his great big paws upon the doorstep of our lives. He was a big red Doberman with a head the size of a basketball, the face of an angel, and a temperament more tolerant than any earthly being. About Rusty, it could honestly be said, "If he didn't touch your soul, then you had no soul to touch."

Now, where do we begin the odyssey of Rusty Ranger Garwood, Big Red?

Our family was about to embark on a huge undertaking; a venture that would span five years of hard work, long hours and give us our fill of the best premium ice cream ever made. Daughter Gigi, had taken an after school job at a neighborhood Baskin Robbins 31 flavors ice cream store in a shopping center quite close to our home. As the weeks progressed, she would often mention that the owner was seeking someone to purchase the franchise. Whatever possessed us to even inquire about this opportunity I will never know. Our forte was the music business, giving private lessons to aspiring young musicians and teaching them the joy of playing a musical instrument. We knew nothing about ice cream or the retail business of selling it, but for some unexplained reason the dream was pursued and like an avalanche barreling down the mountainside, this project soon had a life of its own.   Ben and I were interviewed by the

Baskin Robbin's corporate leaders and were subsequently approved as suitable storeowners. We then proceeded to take the necessary training on how to operate and manage a store. We were tutored in the complexities of ordering ice cream and supplies, gleaned the necessary knowledge of payroll and taxes, and mastered the ability to turn eager hirelings into effective clerks.

On the more creative side we absorbed the art of cake decorating, became expert custom pie makers and acquired the knack of reproducing glamorous desserts while dishing up sundaes and scooping the best looking ice cream cone this city has ever seen.

The day finally arrived when the names were all signed on the bottom line, keys were exchanged, and we were now the new and very inexperienced owners of this busy little ice cream parlor that catered to the whims of all who entered. We became connoisseurs of Pralines and Cream, World Class Chocolate, Mint Chocolate Chip and the many hundreds of wonderful rotating flavors that drew the masses to our door.

It was a family run business in the most pure form. Mom, Pop, and three teenage children labored alongside a wonderful variety of high school clerks that worked their hearts out for us. Our years with Baskin Robbins could be a book by itself, and it comprised five of the most remarkable years of my life. I loved working with my children. At a time when most pull away from their parents as part of their high school independence, ours were stuck to me like glue. We were together day and night, in the slack times and during those busy rushes when everyone came through our doors craving their favorite flavor of fun. It was a time in our relationship when I went from being just 'mom' to becoming their employer and a friend. We laughed and played while eating more ice cream than anyone could have deemed possible. It was hard work but great fun and even to this day, when we mention the store, humorous stories and laughter abound.

Ben was still teaching school but would fill his evenings and weekends with creative cake decorating and rotating the holiday themes that added so much excitement to our store. We never would have considered this business venture without the help of our dear, and lifelong friend, Jeanne. She and I opened that very first day and with the gumption of pioneer women, faced the seasonal challenges of Easter bunny roll cakes, Thanksgiving pies, Christmas Yule logs and scooping ice cream that was often frozen harder than a rock. There were times when only a banana split could cover the stress of the day, but we plowed through the ups and downs of hectic holidays and survived America's crazy obsession with ice cream.

A well-run establishment needed the owners on the premises and we firmly believed in that solid business philosophy, so as a result, we found ourselves working the store from early morning until long into the evenings. On the home hearth there were just the two Dobermans, Samson the Mighty, an older black male and Nurse Cody, our red female. They were each other's constant companions and with less human contact, they began to rely heavily upon one another for comfort and support.

Our lovely Cody began to lose weight and nothing we could feed her would regain her healthful physique. It developed to the point where we consulted Dr. Deere and he gently informed us of her fate. There was a fast growing cancer consuming her and all his knowledgeable skill could not stop the out of control invader. It was a hopeless situation and he advised us that by ending her life then, she would not suffer the painful effects of this devastating disease. We trusted his expertise, for Dr.

Deere had seen the living skeletons of animals that had been left to battle to the end of their days and he knew our sweet Cody deserved that last gift of love by ending her life before being overcome by painful suffering.

We said our good-byes, cried our river of tears and faced the weeks ahead with the numbness of the walking dead. We all mourned her passing, but especially poor Sam, who now spent much of his day and night in confusing solitude. He was there when we brought her home as a puppy and nothing in his reasoning could explain why she should leave him so soon.

Month after month passed and our hearts were finally on the mend when the very nagging thought of getting another dog started to control my mind. It was a completely irrational move to add another pet to our very hectic lives, but however foolish, it filled my waking hours. I guess I just needed another dog and seeing Sam pining from loneliness compounded the situation, so eventually I convinced Ben that the time was right indeed.

The newspaper ad said, "Big boned Dobermans, male and female, Black or Red, $65.00," and gave the address of a rural area about an hour away. We made an appointment to go out one evening to view the prospective pups. Glory be, Oh happy day! We were going to get a puppy for Sam (and me)!

The next night Ben and I headed out into the country to scout out our newest family member. We drove up to a pleasant looking farmhouse in the middle of a long rural route and met the farmer we had contacted on the phone. He took us out to the picturesque red barn and introduced us to the family of puppies he was anxious to sell. They were a mass of sprawled, slumbering, pudgy butterballs all snuggled on top of one another, purebred and country raised. Nothing is cuter than a litter of young pups, all sleepy and limp with their over-sized feet and innocent baby faces. I just wanted to say, "We will take them all", but the voice of reason reminded me why we were there. One black female was our goal and the farmer drew out the three remaining black puppies from the nesting area in the far back corner of the building.

The girls had just eaten, were very drowsy and just wanted to go back to their straw bed filled with the warm bodies of their siblings. They were not about to put on a show for the city folks that coddled them. While we were pondering our decision, one young, red male broke free from his confinement and raced over to greet us.

He was a big boy, full of fire, and a classic show-off. Trying to concentrate was becoming more difficult as our attention was constantly being drawn to him chasing a cat and looking back at us to see if we had been impressed. Unexpectedly, he suddenly raced out the open door, while slipping and sliding on the loose straw. We asked the farmer if he was concerned that the rambunctious redhead might run off. "He always comes back," was his weary reply, as at that precise moment the Red Baron did return... skidding to a halt in front of us with his laughing eyes ablaze.

This red boy was super friendly, extremely charming and every fiber within him cried out, "Take me, take me." We just couldn't help but call him Rusty, as no other name could have ever fit him more completely. He was copper-colored, floppy-eared, bigheaded, huge boned, and had the comic timing of a veteran vaudeville performer. But we had come with our minds made up and a male pup was not on our agenda.

The deal was made and as we hoisted his sister up into our van, that little red fellow just watched us drive away, his hopes still with us until we were out of sight. On the way home we sweet-talked and petted our new puppy, and daughter Ginger, had the honor of bestowing the name of Scoopy upon her. She was a good traveler who melted into the soft and warm covers we had bundled around her and from that moment forward this young dog never again experienced the sensation of cold or hardship. As the journey progressed, our conversation would continually return to the farm and that silly boy dog. Wasn't he funny and didn't he just love people? What a character! We had our dog, the position was filled, so why could we not get the last vision of that terribly disappointed puppy face out of our minds?

The next day was filled with putting up blockades, spreading newspapers and playing with Scoopy when I got an urgent call from Ben. He could not stand it any more and told me to call the farmer and tell him to hold that red puppy for us, we would be out to pick him up that evening.

Two dogs, a boy and girl. Now, that made a lot of sense, but it was a decision we never regretted. We returned the next night and as the transaction was being completed the farmer told us that the litter originally had thirteen puppies. Then, unexpectedly, the young dogs began disappearing and he could not determine what misfortune had befallen them. By the time four of them were missing, he finally figured it out. In the back corner of the barn where the puppies had their bed, there was a loose board in the outer siding of the structure. Very late at night, those sleeping pups would sense a tiny hand groping among them and the fattest, closest or perhaps most docile would feel those little fingers take a vice like grip and drag them through that unsecured board. Out into the harsh reality of the darkened night one can only imagine the horror of facing that devil-eyed monster wearing a bandit's disguise and the savage, bone-crushing end to a very short and sheltered life.

The night we took Scoopy and left that big

handsome pup, the ravaging raccoon had stuck again. Good hearted Rusty may well have known the probing of the shoplifter's hand and because of his nature he would not have mistrusted a touch that was so very like the kind stroke of a human. The molester may have even been gentle or caressing, so as not to raise suspicion or cause alarm as to the real reason why he was there.

But on this dark eve, the farmer was not to be fooled again by the hungry outlaw. He waited long into the night and watched as the thieving varmint silently sneaked up to the corner of the building and methodically rotated the splinted board to the side. There was no hurry, just the slow deliberate move of one who rather enjoyed his hunting expedition. First one hand, then the other passed into the opening and while the farmer watched, a sly smile spread across the poacher's face. A gentle tug, a smooth wiggle and a fat, sassy red pup was exposed to the night air.

The farmer had seen enough and the explosion from that double barrel shotgun sent a loud, clear message to any other night marauder who thought they could outsmart man. The coon went hurtling backward and the puppy scampered inward through the opening as it burrowed back into the safety of the pile of sleeping comrades. His life had been spared and even though he never knew exactly what had happened, he would forevermore relate to that terrifying experience whenever he smelled the strong odor of gunpowder.

Perhaps it was because Rusty never forgot that he was the intended tasty morsel that night, but he was one dog that was ultra sensitive to any confrontation or agitation. If there were a thunder claps or a voice raised in excitement, he would head for the nearest closet to hide from his worst nightmare which was perhaps a pair of creepy little hands that might drag him back into those horrendous moments of his youth.

So began our life with the dog that had only a stub for a tail, a great big *bubber* nose, a tremendous sense of humor and whose entire purpose in life was to please. Scoopy and Rusty were our first Dobermans who did not have their ears trimmed into that typical pointed, up-tight Mr. Spock look. We did not desire that sinister appearance of the breed, but preferred the softer hound dog expression –a face framed by huge, flapping, floppy, silky ears.

Brother and sister only separated from each other by one day, but as different as two dogs could be. Scoopy was a bit of a destructionist as she demolished every unattended shoe, pulled buttons off of clothes, barked at neighbors and had an attitude that meter readers dreadfully respected. But to us, she was a 'pillow princess' and only a mountain of foam rubber was soft enough for her majesty to recline upon. She was a good dog, but rather introverted and not one to seek constant praise or adoration.

Rusty, the classic extrovert, never gave us one moment of trouble, was too conscientious to chew what was not his and always tried to do the right thing. He was the virtuous Gandhi of the neighborhood; never meeting a person he didn't like and peacefully accepted every stray that entered our door. It didn't matter if it was a dog, cat, bird, mouse, spider or squirrel. He would let a sleepy cat prop up against him and use his tummy as a pillow, allow birds to touchdown upon his back as their makeshift landing strip and wash the faces of hobo dogs that dropped by for a handout.

Early on in Rusty's life there was an episode that will forever stand out in my memory. I had finished my shift at the store and came home to let the pups that slept in our bedroom during the day-- outside to romp and play.

Scoopy was usually to be found lying on her padded throne and Rusty would be clenching his pillow as if it were a pacifier. He would not chew, rather just clamp down and gently embrace it in his mouth while his face displayed a picturesque expression of contentment. Vet Deere said many critters had this habit and his explanation was that perhaps they had been weaned too early and missed the comfort of their mother, so they used the bit of cloth as a surrogate mom. Rusty was a mama's boy indeed, so a pillow for a security blanket was just accepted as part of his sensitive, easygoing charm.

When they returned from outside that afternoon, I noticed that a huge mass of frothy saliva was dripping down the side of Rusty's mouth. My instantaneous reaction was that he had contacted rabies or distemper and I tensed at handling a potentially dangerous situation. The mystery was that Rusty did not appear sick or suffering any malaise, but actually was quite happy and playful. He wagged and wiggled while a huge glob of drool dripped off his chin. I looked into a pair of bright shiny eyes, felt his cool, moist nose and was baffled as there was no display of threatening temperament like the nasty dog, Cujo, we had just recently seen in a movie about the mayhem of a St. Bernard with rabies.

Ben was not home from school yet and the children were nowhere to be found. It was just this big hunk of a potentially rabid puppy and me. My mind raced through the numerous immunizations that Rusty had just received. Was rabies among them or did that series come later when the dog was a bit more mature? What if the raccoon that had been menacing the litter of pups was afflicted and Rusty had been bitten or scratched by that savage beast?

The next scenario that went through my poor tortured mind was a story told to us by Fred, the husband of co-worker Jeanne. He had extended his hand to a stray pup while living in downtown Chicago years earlier and the dog nipped him then disappeared into the huge mass of commuters. Knowing the horrors of hydrophobia, he did not hesitate to take the series of injections to prevent the malady. The first series of the twenty-six shots was administered into one armpit— the second under the other and as huge golf ball sized swellings soon developed, the remaining shots had to be inserted into the tender region of his stomach. He would comically demonstrate his predicament; arms extended straight out while cramped over in a crouched position, as he could neither sit nor stand without immense discomfort until the vaccine had been absorbed into his system.

My brow by now must have been furrowed with concern. I dreaded the agony of shots but the alternative of rabies was even more horrific. Hollywood movies had covered that subject quite well in my memory. I could recall it all so vividly-- the unfortunate bite victim chained to a stake, begging for water and then violently repelled at the sight of it. Writhing in pain, moaning in agony, drowning in sweat and then finally dying in a dramatic, heart-wrenching scene as the victim gathers all remaining strength for a theatrical good-bye.

I was dumbfounded in terror, grief stuck, and paralyzed by fear. All the while Rusty was slobbering foam and chasing Scoopy through the house, spit and slime flying in sporadic spurts. He finally collapsed in my lap, oozed some extra big bubbles and looked at me with the intoxicated eyes of a sailor home on leave.

I woefully looked down upon my poor dying pup. Tears welled up in my eyes as I held him close when I detected a faint trace of the smell of cocoa butter. It was an odor that I was very comfortable with and it seemed odd that dreaded rabies should smell so pleasant. Then for some unexplained reason, I pried open that gurgling mass and discovered the source of the bubble machine. An entire bar of soap was wedged up in the roof of Rusty's mouth causing his salivary glands to pump out great gallons of water to try to flood the unwanted alien out. The case had been solved and a great Sherlock Holmes smile spread across my face. Rusty-darling was a puppy with a severe soap fetish and whenever the bar was missing, we always knew where to look. Just follow the trail of floating bubbles to the boy with the silly, foaming grin.

Rusty had such an easy going nature that Dr. Deere suspected he must surely have had a low functioning thyroid gland, but it was more than just slow metabolism that made Rusty who he was. He was just a good soul, plain and simple. We would bring him up to the store in the evenings and he would greet all customers with such panache that sometimes they would seem to forget why they had come. Rusty just enjoyed people, and his very presence seemed to be reason enough for two complete strangers to strike up a conversation.

Our children would often ask us, "Don't you ever feel the slightest bit embarrassed when we tell people of how you pamper Rusty?" Nope, not one bit. He was like a little boy to us, the younger brother that Clint never had and if we spoiled him it was because he gave so much back to us.

Rusty's daily schedule consisted of a bagel first thing in the morning, one cheese stick mid-day, an oatmeal cookie before bed and Milk Duds whenever he could get them. Early on in his life he developed an eating disorder and no, it was not because of all those little extra treats. He simply stopped eating his dog food and nothing we could do would persuade him to re-consider that decision. Doc Deere, patiently on call for our many concerns, said not to worry, for after a day or so he would get hungry enough and plow into his food with gusto. We waited; one day, two days, then three days passed. Rusty's sad eyes said, "Mom, I can't do it, I just can't eat," so I sat down on the floor with him, a spoon in hand and fed him bites from his bowl. The next day and every day after that for the rest of his life, this scenario was to become routine. Rusty, opening his mouth like a toddler and me spooning in the food. After he finished his entire meal I would proudly announce to Ben, "Rusty ate his supper like a man." Good boy Rusty! Just like a man.

One by one, the children marched off to college and when the last had left our fold, we sold the store and our hectic lifestyle began to slow down. With this new life we experienced more freedom and added a trip to the walking trail as part of our daily ritual. Rusty loved that part of the day and 'Go-Park-Play' was how we described it. He would run like a deer in the fields, ears flapping as he crashed through the tall prairie grass in hopes of surprising some unsuspecting bunny or bird. It was great fun for him and clearly a highlight of his life.

As the years progressed, the ravages of time began to take its deadly toll. Our dear, sweet Scoopy was only seven years old when she developed disabling congestive heart failure and we sadly watched as this malicious disease heartlessly drained the spark of vitality from her. When it reached the stage where she could no longer recline upon those beloved downy pillows but was forced to stand because of fluid buildup in her lungs, we took our little princess to Vet Deere to administer the final injection that would help ease her from a painful life.

After an entire lifetime together, Rusty had lost his sister, littermate and best friend. His sadness began to drain the youth from his spirit and in depressed agony he wandered aimlessly through the trails of our wooded yard searching hopelessly for the one who would never return to him. Even old friend Sam could not help his dear buddy Rusty. Being twelve years old, he had become the *grand old man* and had long forgotten the art of romping or racing with another dog. Sam's own course of exit had started many years earlier as huge cancerous tumors had begun to invade his body feeding on the meat from his bones and protein from his once gleaming and beautiful coat. Within months from Scoopy's demise, Sam was taken for that last farewell ride when he could no longer endure what that mean spirited disease had wreaked upon his body.

So, where there had once been three longtime friends, a trio of musketeers in the canine club, there now remained one single, solitary member left alone drowning in overwhelming grief. Rusty no longer ran or scouted like he had always done but acted old, depressed, and uninterested in life. It was too much sadness in so short a time span and we were frightened that Rusty would give up the will to live as a result. Broken hearts have taken many a healthy soul to the other side of life and we could not stand by to watch that befall our mournful friend.

Several months earlier Ben had clipped a picture from our local newspaper of a most enchanting looking dog. It was a German shorthaired pointer with a face that was so captivating that Ben placed it on his bedside table. This little bird dog seemed to beckon us from afar and suddenly the reason became perfectly clear. He was to be the puppy that would bring our Rusty back to us and become the much-needed medicine that we all craved. We named him, Rowdy Rodeo Rawhide Rusty Ranger Jr. and from the very beginning we called him 'Rusty's puppy'.

Upon being brought home and presented to Rusty, the sorrowful look left those mourning eyes like the sun shaking free from a black thundercloud. In no time at all, a twinkle of laughter began to replace his mournful expression. Old Rip Van Winkle had finally awakened and that slow moving, bone weary creature that had become our Rusty was now up and sniffing this wiggling, wagging silly little scamp of a pup. An excited little bark from the newcomer suggested, "Hey, let's go play, big boy," and so they did, running, romping, wrestling, chasing, darting, hiding and then the delightful fun of finding.

We cheered the change that had come over Rusty as the two dogs rough and tumbled their way over the hills and valleys of our yard. Rusty, with a glad heart became mentor, parent, big brother and best friend to this bright young charge. Instant love was their very first emotion and linking bond. Rusty and Rowdy, one nine years and the other eight months, but both now so full of energy and pep we could see no age difference between them. Running buddies, sleep partners, couch potatoes, chipmunk chasers, and two of the happiest dogs we ever had the honor to know.

We seldom missed a day bringing Rusty and Rowdy out to the field to exercise and along about Rusty's eleventh year we began to notice that a cough was starting to develop after each run. He was in such great physical shape; it did not concern us until we noticed he was out of breath at even the slightest exertion. Discussions with the vet, various breeders and other dog owners confirmed the diagnosis that somehow Rusty had contracted a fungus that was consuming his lung capacity at an alarming rate. We agonized that perhaps by letting him run the field or woods his heavy panting may have placed the deadly fungus deeper into vulnerable lungs.

The treatment to save his life would have cost thousands of dollars and on a very young dog, survival might have been possible, but Rusty's age and the hold the disease had on his delicate support system was too far along to reverse. We were basically told to go home and prepare for the end. Rusty could no longer race through those fields and even a mild walk winded him tremendously. Every breath was a labor and often times he would choose standing up over laying down as the only way to secure enough air. The lack of oxygen to his body caused his back legs to weaken and occasionally they would buckle causing him to collapse. We struggled with the decision of putting him to sleep, but simply could not bear to say good-bye to our good friend and we knew that he was not ready to leave us either.

Ben and I just wanted him to die at home and even though many times before we had taken a dog in for euthanasia when the disease began threatening the quality of their life, Rusty was different. He was so close to us it was like having a parent ask not to be placed in a nursing home and the promise just had to be kept. He had never been away from us before and even the smallest separation always scared him, so we just could not imagine taking him to some frightening, strange place to end his life.

The memory of the night he died is as clear as if it happened yesterday. During that day, Rusty had many coughing spells and was becoming weary with the struggle of living. Ben reluctantly had to go to a meeting, so I stayed home with the dogs. About eight o'clock Rusty asked to go outside and even in his weakened condition, there was still a pride in his tidy bathroom habits. Once finished, his back legs folded and down to the ground he fell. I helped him back into the house and just inside the patio door an angel called him home and Rusty gave up that well fought battle he had waged for the last year. There were some difficult moments as he struggled for breath, but basically it was a fast, easy passing. I told him we loved him and that he had given his best. After a sigh his soul was gone. Our good, gentle boy never more to run upon the earth that he so joyfully cherished. Every night before falling asleep, Ben had the habit of saying to Rusty, "See you in the morning, big boy," and that is what I whispered to him as his spirit departed his body.

One of the most difficult realities of any animal's passing is having to walk out of the veterinary clinic and leave your best friend behind for the doctor to dispose of. Years later we found the most wonderful solution to this very difficult situation.

Ben was invited to serve on the Board of Directors of Arlington Cemetery here in our hometown of Rockford, Illinois. It is a peaceful, lovely locale and the ideal habitat to call our final resting-place. But it was the pet cemetery nestled within the confines of the park-like setting that really finalized our decision.

The animal cemetery is laid out in three distinct areas: the bronze makers, the marble stones and the upright monuments. The area is so ablaze with decorative memorials that one cannot help but be drawn from one marker to the next. The tenderness of the heartfelt inscriptions etched upon those headstones would cause anyone understanding such a loss to bow a head and shed a tear.

This sacred parcel of land is bordered by a gentle hillside on the south and surrounded by wooded terrain on all other sides. Something about that undeveloped hill of thistle weed seemed to beckon to Ben and me, suggesting we create a monument of flowers that would add to the ambiance of this final resting ground of so many beloved souls.

After securing the blessing of the board and generous donations from local businesses, we grappled with this wild, unruly hillside-- clearing, leveling, hoeing, weeding, and mulching. Then with the dedicated help from close friend, Jeanne Marler, we tackled the planting, daily watering and hopeful watching as the wasteland developed into a garden of glory. And as we worked, we were gifted with a surprise bonus of forging friendships with those who came (sometimes daily) to spend a moment in memory with their departed pet friends.

The garden was christened 'Rainbow Ridge' and now the bounty of multi-colored flowers radiating their beauty is a tribute and thank-you to those animal companions that have passed over, but will never be forgotten. It is where I plan to place our animals-- surrounded by flowers and tended with perpetual care.

This was an endeavor we believe to have been divinely inspired and having been a part of the creation of Rainbow Ridge brings me great contentment and comfort.

As sure as I am sitting here engulfed in these sad memories of Rusty, I firmly believe that if no dogs, cats or cherished animals are allowed in heaven, well, then it wouldn't be the paradise that most of us have always envisioned. Our pets, with their unconditional love and devotion are sometimes the only ones that make life tolerable on this cruel old planet when the qualities of kindness and compassion have been harshly cast aside by the cutthroat competitors of the human race. Spending eternity without animals would be like a world without a reason to smile. No amount of revelry could make up for the loss of those very special elements in our lives...our favorite friends.

Many people do not choose to replace an animal after an especially sad ending by saying they cannot go through the grief again and as a result just shut off that compassionate part of their soul. All those years of laughter and joy gifted to them by their pet are now downplayed as unimportant and the episode of death takes center stage, overshadowing all. But if we hide in self-imposed caves dreading the dark sadness of the inevitable departure, we will never again live in love's light found by sharing life.

If we had given up on all other dogs after Cody's passing, we would not have had the gift of sharing our lives with Rusty, and that would have been a tragedy of the most momentous proportions. What did we get for loving him? Well, we were given an insight into a truly remarkable character that saw no flaw in anyone-- rather the bright and shining potential in everyone. He brought out the best in all of us and every memory of him is so dazzling it just re-kindles those feelings that we worried might disappear when our arms could no longer embrace him.

It has now been many years without Rusty. New dogs Rowdy, Bubba, and Dexter share our journey and run the very fields that he so loved. But Rusty is out there among us, in pure spirit, big ears flapping and laughing face all aglow. He directs the sweet summer breeze to lap our cheek and turns on that tiny sunbeam to highlight a hidden patch of wildflowers that we had never before noticed. He lives through us in the good will we feel toward all God's creatures and we are proud to pay homage to Rusty's memory by spreading his philosophy of kindness and grace. His death was not a good-bye but rather an 'aloha', the enchanting Hawaiian word that eliminates any boundaries between hello and farewell.

Aloha, Rusty Ranger. You made a huge difference in our lives and as surely as the great Caretaker is looking down upon us all, we will *see you in the morning, Big Boy.*

Find this and other Tarbutton Press titles at your local bookstore or order direct from Tarbutton Press.

Quick Order Form

Fax Orders: (616) 329-3242

Email Orders: http://www.tarbuttonpress.com

Postal Orders:

Tarbutton Press

6749 S. Westnedge Ave..,

Suite K., PMB 261,

Portage, MI, 49002

Please send the following books:

Tell Me Something Pretty:$17.95x _____ = $_____
Paperback, by Gale O'Bryant

Gumshoe Girls: $17.95 x _____ = $_____
Hardcover, by Gale O'Bryant

The Hierophant: $.12.95 x_____ =$_____
Paperback, by T.R. Hammack

Gargoyle Tears: $12.95 x_____ =$_____
Paperback, by JV Harlee

                                    Subtotal $_____

Shipping $3 for first book,   Shipping $_____
$2.00 for each additional book

                                    Total $_____

American Humane Association

63 Inverness Dr. East

Englewood, CO 80112-5117

Yes! I want to help the American Humane Association build more caring and humane communities. Enclosed is my tax-deductible gift of:

$25 $50 $100 $500   Other $ _____

☐   ☐   ☐   ☐

Please make your check payable to American Humane Association. You can also make a contribution by calling toll-free 1-866-AHA-1877 or online at www.americanhumane.org.

Name: _____

Address: _____

_____

DISCOVER   MASTERCARD   VISA

☐   ☐   ☐

Expiration Date _____

Credit Card No._____

Signature:_____ _____

All charges must be accompanied by authorized signature

Phone No.:

Printed in the United States
31378LVS00002B/103-177